FREE TO BE THIN

COOKBOOK

FREE TO BE THIN

COOKBOOK

NEVA COYLE

BETHANY HOUSE PUBLISHERS
MINNEAPOLIS, MINNESOTA 55438

Neva Coyle

ISBN 0-87123-255-3
Copyright © 1982
Neva Coyle
All Rights Reserved

Published by Bethany House Publishers
A Division of Bethany Fellowship, Inc.
6820 Auto Club Road, Minneapolis, Minnesota 55438
Printed in the United States of America

A Note From Neva

What's for supper? What shall I cook for myself?

Questions that are asked every day are now answered in this cookbook. It is a very special cookbook. It was written by people who have been on the Overeaters Victorious program and have asked and answered these very questions for themselves.

In this book we have taken the favorite recipes of many OVers and put them together to make them available to you.

It is with our best wishes that we present this collection to you. You will find many opportunities to use your own favorite seasonings and make the dishes uniquely your own.

We give these recipes to you with our blessings.

As always,
Because of Jesus,

Neva Coyle

Contributors

Mickey Beerman
La Vonne Berg
Joy Class
Charlotte Coe
Neva Coyle
Maureen Dahl
Myrlene Diekhoff
Mary Guffin
Kathy Hiemforth
Mary Ann Holbrook
April Hollingsworth
Esme' Kepple
Kathy Megazzi
Diane Meyer
Dorothy Michels
Jane Nasan
Anne Phillips
Karen Priddy
Nancy Shea
Kathy Walker
Barb Wilkins

Contents

Recommended Diet Guideline

The Simple Way to Eat

(For most women and small-frame men)	(For most men and large-frame women)
Breakfast High Vitamin C fruit Protein food (choose one) 2 ounces cottage or pot cheese 1 ounce hard cheese 1 egg 2 ounces cooked or canned fish 8 ounces skim milk Bread or cereal, whole grain (choose one) 　1 slice whole-grain bread 　¾ cup ready-to-eat cereal 　½ cup cooked cereal Beverage	**Breakfast** High Vitamin C fruit Protein food (choose one) 　2 ounces cottage or pot cheese 　1 ounce hard cheese 　1 egg 　2 ounces cooked or canned fish 　8 ounces skim milk Bread or cereal, whole grain (choose one) 　2 slices whole-grain bread 　1½ cups ready-to-eat cereal 　½ cup cooked cereal Beverage
Lunch Protein food (choose one) 　2 ounces fish, poultry, or lean meat 　4 ounces cottage or pot cheese 　2 ounces hard cheese 　1 egg 　2 level tablespoons peanut butter Bread—2 slices whole grain Vegetables—raw or cooked, except potato or substitute Fruit—1 serving Beverage	**Lunch** Protein food (choose one) 　2 ounces fish, poultry, or lean meat 　4 ounces cottage or pot cheese 　2 ounces hard cheese 　1 egg 　2 level teaspoons peanut butter Bread—2 slices whole grain Vegetables—raw or cooked, except potato or substitute Fruit—1 serving Beverage
Dinner Protein food (choose one) 　4 ounces cooked fish, poultry, or lean meat Vegetables—cooked and raw 　High Vitamin A—choose from Food Facts 　Potato or substitute from Food Facts 　Other vegetables—you may eat responsibly Fruit—1 serving Beverage	**Dinner** Protein food (choose one) 　6 ounces cooked fish, poultry, or lean meat Vegetables—cooked and raw 　High Vitamin A—choose from Food Facts 　Potato or substitute from Food Facts 　Other vegetables—you may eat responsibly Fruit—1 serving Beverage
Other Daily Foods Fat—choose 3 from Food Facts Milk—2 cups (8 ounces each) skim or substitute from Food Facts	**Other Daily Foods** Fat—choose 6 from Food Facts Milk—2 cups (8 ounces each) skim or substitute from Food Facts

REMEMBER TO MEASURE QUANTITIES OF EACH SERVING AND ACCOUNT FOR EVERY CALORIE!

Simple Way to Shop

To assist you in planning ahead, use the following checklist as a reminder while you are making up your shopping list. For each person you are cooking for who is following the **Simple Way to Eat**, you will need the quantities listed per week.

Checklist

Check	One Week / One Person
_____	7 servings high vitamin C fruits
_____	14 servings other fruits
_____	7 servings breakfast proteins
_____	7 servings lunch proteins
_____	7 servings dinner proteins
_____	7-21 slices or servings bread or other grain products
_____	14 servings favorite vegetables eaten raw and in salads
_____	Up to 14 servings vegetables eaten cooked
_____	7 servings potato or substitutes
_____	Beverages—non-caloric and/or others
_____	21 portions fats (Consult the **Food Facts**.)
_____	16 milk servings (Consult the **Food Facts**.)

Notes

_____

_____

_____

_____

_____

_____

_____

_____

Sweetening

It is often necessary to sweeten our recipes to make them more tasty and appetizing. The Bible makes several statements that we should keep in mind here:

1. **Colossians 2:16**: No one is to pass judgment in regard to food.
2. **1 Corinthians 3:17**: God says your body is holy.
3. **1 Corinthians 6:19,20**: God says that your body is the temple or dwelling place of the Holy Spirit. You are not your own, but have been purchased with a price—a very high price, Jesus. So we purpose in everything to glorify God in our bodies.
4. **Hebrews 12:13**: We are told to make smooth, easy paths for our feet—not to make it hard on ourselves. This could mean that sometimes we should make some of our good nutritional food more palatable by sweetening it.

Now, in light of this, we have included the terms "sweetener" and "sweeten to taste" in some recipes. You will have to decide for yourself what you will use to sweeten your dishes. We have not included the calorie count of the sweeteners in these recipes because it will vary with the type you use. Be sure to consult your calorie counter or the sweetener container for the correct count and add it to your particular recipe.

One suggestion: Try using fructose on fruit dishes that require sweetening. It does not mask the fruit flavor or leave an aftertaste like artificial sweetener does, and it is lower in calories than either sugar or honey.

One more suggestion: Considering just how sweet you already are, why not try to educate your tongue to unsweetened dishes several times a week and work on developing a taste for them?

Simple Nutrition

Build Meals Around These
FOUR IMPORTANT FOOD GROUPS

Milk Group (Use daily.)

3 or more glasses milk—children; 4 or more—teenagers (smaller glasses for some children under 9)
2 or more glasses—adults
4 or more glasses—pregnant women
4 or more glasses—nursing mothers
(a glass = 8 ounces or ¼ quart of milk)

Needs of some younger children may be met by smaller servings; i.e., a 6-ounce glass may replace an 8-ounce glass.

These quantities of milk provide about ¾ of the day's calcium recommended for good nutrition.

Milk is our main source of calcium in foods. For calcium...
1 slice American cheese (1 ounce) = ¾ glass milk
½ cup creamed cottage cheese = ⅓ glass milk
½ cup (¼ pint) ice cream = ¼ glass milk

Milk also contributes fine quality protein, vitamins—especially riboflavin and vitamin A—and many other nutrients.

For children, 3 glasses of milk supply about ½ the protein recommended daily and all or almost all the riboflavin.

For adults, 2 glasses of milk supply about ¼ the protein and about ½ the riboflavin.

Skim milk lacks whole milk's fat and vitamin A (unless fortified); other food values are the same, calories less.

One glass of skim milk plus 1 scant tablespoon of butter equals the food values of whole milk.

Butter supplies milk's flavorful and easily digested fat along with its vitamin A.

Use milk as a beverage and in cooking—in hot cereals, milk soups, white sauces, puddings, and custards. Pour on fruit, cereal, and puddings.

The combination of milk with cereal or bread is excellent, especially in meals where little or no meat or eggs are served. The proteins in milk make those in cereals and bread more useful in the body.

Meat Group (Use 2 or more servings daily.)

Meat, fish, poultry, eggs, or cheese—with dry beans, peas, nuts, or peanut butter as alternates

Use amounts of these foods to supply at least as much protein as that in 4 ounces of cooked lean meat (about ⅓ pound raw).

Teenagers, pregnant women, and nursing mothers need larger amounts of these foods.

Good practices to follow are
An egg a day or at least 3-5 a week
Liver, heart, kidney, or sweetbread about once a week
Other kinds of meat, fish, poultry or cheese 4-5 or more times a week
With dried beans, peas, nuts, or peanut butter, serve milk or cheese. The animal protein makes the vegetable protein more useful in the body.

Foods in the meat group are counted on to supply about ½ the protein recommended daily for good nutrition.

Two servings for an adult might be, for example,
   1 medium serving meat (3 ounces, cooked) + 1 egg
Choose combinations from the following which are about equal in amount of
   protein:
   1 ounce cooked lean meat, poultry, or fish
   1 egg
   1 slice (1 ounce) cheese, American or Swiss
   2 tablespoons (1 ounce) creamed cottage cheese
   2 tablespoons (1 ounce) peanut butter
   ½ cup cooked dried beans or peas
Eggs and meat, especially liver, are important for iron, also for B-vitamins. Pork
   supplies large amounts of the B-vitamin thiamine. The legumes—dried
   beans, peas, nuts—are good sources of iron and thiamine, but their protein
   should be supplemented with an animal protein.

Vegetables & Fruits (Use 4 or more servings daily.)

**Include a dark green leafy or deep yellow vegetable or yellow fruit at
least 3-4 times a week for vitamin A; a citrus fruit, or tomatoes, or other
good source of vitamin C, every day.**

Use other vegetables and fruits for variety as well as their minerals, vitamins,
   and roughage.

Use potatoes frequently for all these food values plus food energy.

Use fresh, canned, or frozen vegetables and fruits.

Save food values and flavors of vegetables by cooking quickly in small amount
   of water.

Dried fruits are valuable for iron.

A serving is ½ cup or more.

Foods in this group should supply over ½ the vitamin A and all of the vitamin C
   recommended daily for good nutrition.

These Are About Equal in Vitamin C.

Broccoli, chard	1 medium orange, ¾ cup juice
All greens	½ grapefruit, ¾ cup juice
Kale, spinach	2 medium tomatoes, 2 cups juice
Carrots	½ large cantaloupe
Sweet potatoes	1 cup strawberries
Tomatoes	¾ cup broccoli
Cantaloupe, apricots	1½ cups cabbage, raw, shredded

Breads & Cereals (Use 4 or more servings daily.)

Use enriched or whole-grain products. Check labels!

Choose from breads, cooked and ready-to-eat cereals, cornmeal, crackers,
   grits, spaghetti and macaroni, noodles, rice, quick breads and other baked
   goods if made with whole-grain or enriched flour.

A serving is 1 slice bread; ½-¾ cup cereal.

Foods in this group supply valuable amounts of protein, iron, several B-vitamins,
   and food energy.

Cereals cooked and/or served with milk and breads made with milk are
   improved in quality of protein as well as quantity of protein, minerals, and
   vitamins.

Additional Foods...
The foods recommended form the foundation for a good diet.

In general, use smaller servings for young children; more or larger servings may be needed by teenagers, pregnant and lactating women.

Most nutrient needs are met by the amounts of foods suggested in **Food Facts**. Special attention must be given to food sources of iron for children, teenagers, pregnant and lactating women. Liver, eggs, meat, legumes, dried fruit, dark green leafy vegetables, enriched or whole-grain breads and cereals are good iron sources.

More food for energy, calories, is usually required. The amount varies with age, size, and activity. Food from the four food groups helps to achieve an adequate diet.

Calorie-restricted diets can be pleasing and satisfying when energy comes mostly from foods in these four groups.

Some source of vitamin D should be included for infants and children, pregnant and lactating women, and adults getting little sunshine. Good sources are vitamin D milk, fish liver oils, and direct sunshine.

Menu Ideas

This section is only geared to helping you to be more creative. It is not a day-by-day plan that you have to follow, nor am I suggesting such. Just let some new ideas brighten your routine.

Breakfasts that Get Your Day Started in Style

"OV"*-Style Pancakes
Blueberries in a compote or spooned over the top of the pancakes
Hot beverage, if desired

Hashbrown Casserole
Grapefruit, lightly drizzled with honey, sprinkled with cinnamon
    and placed under the broiler until bubbly

Spanish Omelet
Oranges sliced crossways
Toast

Sour Cream Scrambled Eggs
Blueberries and green grapes mixed together in a little glass dish
Bran muffin

OV-Style French Toast smothered with sliced strawberries

Fruit Salad made up of:
    Sliced bananas
    Pineapple chunks
    Seedless green grapes
    Whole strawberries
Fruit Sauce (for family only)
    ⅓ can Eagle Brand sweetened condensed milk
    1 teaspoon lemon juice
    1 egg, whipped with fork
(Blend together and serve over fruit.)

Lunch with Middle-of-the-Day Zip

Any of the Pizza entrees served with salad and various raw vegetables and an apple

*OV stands for Overeaters Victorious, a successful weight control organization
  based on principles from the Bible.

FOR A COLD DAY
Slim Jim Chile
Crackers
Baked apple
Hot tea

FOR A HOT DAY
Chicken Salad Slenderizer
French-style green beans tossed cold with low-calorie Italian
    dressing and onion rings
Strawberries and pineapple chunks

Lemon-Baked Chicken
Steamed zucchini, yellow squash, carrots, and cauliflower
Slices tomatoes on a lettuce leaf
Watermelon

Chicken Salad Hawaiian
Bran muffin
Cooked carrots

Dinner Is Bringing the Family Together
It is possible to feed the family on the same program you are on
with very few adjustments as to portion sizes and supplemental
dishes.

Hurry Beef Stew
Green salad with crackers (muffins or toast for the family)
Baked apples

Chicken Cacciatore
Steamed vegetables such as zucchini, cauliflower, etc. For a
    special treat add corn on the cob in 2-inch sections.
Baked potato
Tossed salad or coleslaw
Fresh oranges

Tuna Casserole
French-style green beans
Sliced tomatoes
Carrot sticks
Fresh sliced peaches, heated in the oven until heated through
    and sprinkled with sweetener and cinnamon

Orange Juice Poached Fish
Baked potatoes cut into wedges, brushed with egg white,
sprinkled with Parmesan cheese and paprika prior to baking
Cooked carrots sprinkled with cinnamon and drizzled over so
lightly with honey
Spinach and water chestnut salad
Melon

Hamburger broiled on barbecue grill
Foil-wrapped potatoes baked on barbecue grill
Fresh vegie platter (Include sliced tomatoes.)
Low-calorie cottage cheese, whipped until smooth. Add chives.
Use for vegie dip and/or topping for potato.

Entertaining Ideas

Using the **Simple Way to Eat** for entertaining is not hard at all. Most women's gatherings require some type of refreshment served, and most women are very food- and weight-conscious. So, keep the needs of your guests in mind and plan around them.

Baby showers, bridal showers, and other typical ladies' parties are fun and give us a real opportunity to be feminine and creative in decorating. Some basic advice is to plan the food first and then color-coordinate around that.

When planning the food, take into consideration the time of day and the season of the year. Assuming that the fruits are in season, here is a list of colorful suggestions:

Serve cantaloupe and honeydew balls in small compotes (either crystal or clear plastic). Decorate vanilla wafers by placing a small peach frosting flower on each. Use light green napkins and a peach centerpiece made with silk or fresh carnations in a bud vase. Peach candles would be a striking complement.

Serve pineapple chunks (either canned in their own juice or fresh) with seedless green grapes on a platter or in compotes. Use alternate yellow and light green napkins arranged in a fan pattern on the table and yellow candles with a small bouquet of white daisies as a centerpiece.

Popovers can be made in miniature muffins tins (a child's toy size) and filled with cheese. Serve with an exotic tray of fresh fruit skewered on cocktail toothpicks.

In the fall, apples may be cut into wedges and placed attractively around the edge of a platter filled with yellow and white cheeses cut with cookie cutters. Crackers served in baskets are a nice addition. Use fall-colored or bandana-print napkins.

Fruit compote frozen in plastic cups is simple and yet very elegant. Fruits that work well are blueberries, green grapes, red seedless grapes, strawberries, cantaloupe and honeydew balls, orange, apple and banana slices. Cover each with a mixture of one part orange juice concentrate and three parts sugar-free 7-Up or Fresca. Allow fruit cup to partially thaw before serving. It is an icy-type dessert and very colorful. Pick one color from the fruit and set your table accordingly.

Raw vegetables served with the dips in this cookbook are lovely in color and attractive and fun to arrange. Crackers in various sizes and shapes add an interesting effect. Don't forget to serve cheese sliced thin and cut with cookie cutters. (Save the scraps left around the edges for your own salads and lunches.)

On a cold afternoon or evening try serving hot V-8 juice with a celery stick and lemon wedge in a mug. Again, crackers and cheese and a lovely arrangement of fruit on a plate for help-yourself-style serving create a friendly and warm atmosphere.

Beverages at the Coyle house are kept simple for entertaining: a pot of water, with baskets or bowls containing several kinds of tea bags; instant coffee, both decaffeinated and regular; occasionally low-calorie cocoa mix (store-bought and in envelopes); both sugar and artificial sweetener, and milk in a cream pitcher. Guests help themselves, and there is no messy coffeepot to clean at the end of the evening.

Cold beverages may include apple juice mixed half-and-half with 7-Up to make punch. See other recipes in the **Fruit and Desserts** section of this book.

One of the main things I try to remember when entertaining is that my guests will not be comfortable if I am not. Therefore, I place coasters ahead of time on the living room tables, and often serve from my kitchen bar where I am most comfortable. I use my good crystal, a lace tablecloth, and a centerpiece on occasion. Any table can be made elegant and inviting with a just a little creativity and prayerful thought in advance.

If you will learn to think fruit and vegetables when planning your parties, your guests will appreciate it and not even miss the pies, bars, and cakes. Your preparation time is minimal and your tables will require less accessorizing when you start with already beautiful and colorful fruit and vegetables.

Entertainment Tips

- Make it elegant. Keep it simple.
- Elegance is not the ingredients that go into the dish, but the dish the ingredients go into.
- Cook it the simple way, but serve it in style.

SALADS

Sal...Salat...Salad

The word *salad* is derived from the Latin term *sal* meaning "salt." Its modern meaning probably stems from the Roman practice of dunking raw vegetables and green herbs in salt as a kind of dressing. Later the word *sal* evolved into *salat*, which applied to any vegetable dish, raw or cooked, served with a tart dressing.

Although salads of one sort or another had been served even prior to the time when Romans feasted on salted herbs, it was not until the early 1900s that salads became popular on menus. The French perfected the art of combining herbs and greens with a mixture of seasonings, oil, and vinegar, and claimed inventor's rights—hence the name "French dressing." About a century later Americans became aware of the salad, and that awareness has grown and expanded until now we probably serve more and a greater variety of salads than any other nation.

King Richard II of England was so fond of "salat," as it was known then, that his cook wrote down the directions: "Take parsel, sawge (sage), garlec, chibollas (small onions), leeks, myntes, fenel, ton tresses (watercress)...wash hem clene...myng (mix) hem wel with rawe oile. Lay one vinegar and salt and serve it forth." In 20th-century America, as in 14th-century England, the classic salad dressing called "French" is regularly served.

Salads can be classified into three very broad categories: tossed, arranged, and gelatin. But since imagination and ingenuity are always important ingredients, many salads disregard the boundaries and combine the characteristics of two and sometimes all three of these categories.

Common to almost all salads are the green, leafy vegetables used either as an ingredient, underliner, or garnish. They lend color, flavor, and crisp texture, are low in calories and are generally high in essential nutrients.

Salad Greens

Put color, flavor, and textural interest into salads by using a variety of salad greens. These include chicory (curly endive), Chinese cabbage (celery cabbage), leaf lettuce, Romaine lettuce, head lettuce (iceberg lettuce), escarole (broadleaf endive), Boston lettuce, Bibb lettuce (limestone lettuce), French endive, young spinach leaves, celery tops, watercress, and fresh parsley.

Fresh, crisp greens are essential to salad-making success, so select the best quality available, and clean and refrigerate them as soon as possible after purchase.

First, remove any wilted parts from the salad greens, then wash the greens well in lukewarm water. No, lukewarm water won't wilt them, and it is best for thorough cleaning. After washing, drain the greens on a wire rack, on paper towels, or pat them dry with a soft towel. Greens must be thoroughly dry for attractive salads.

To separate a head of lettuce into cups, cut out the core with the point of a knife. Hold the opening under cold running water until the leaves are forced apart.

Once the greens have been cleaned, store them in the refrigerator in a vegetable crisper or plastic bag to chill and crisp.

Wash parsley and watercress as directed above, but store them in a tightly covered container (a glass jar is convenient).

Serve a salad as an accompaniment to be eaten with the main course or to garnish the meat platter. It can also be served as a first-course appetizer, a main dish, a salad plate, a dessert salad, or party salad.

Salad pointers to be remembered:
1. Use only chilled and crisped salad greens.
2. Greens should never extend beyond the edge of the plate. Excess greenery can dwarf a salad.

3. Try for color, flavor, form, and textural contrast when combining salad ingredients.
4. Always chill canned fruits and vegetables.
5. Drain canned fruits thoroughly on paper towels, vegetables in a sieve.
6. Arrange any salad on a chilled plate or bowl in a simple manner. Avoid a cluttered effect.
7. Combine or arrange salads just before serving for a fresh, appetizing appearance.

Vegetables are low in calories, especially if you limit the amount of salad dressing. Compare the calories in 1 tablespoon of *regular* salad dressing:

	Calories
French dressing	65
Italian dressing	80
Mayonnaise	100
Mayonnaise-type salad dressing	65
Sour cream	25
Yogurt (plain)	10

Main-dish salads can be made from a combination of cooked or raw vegetables, meat, fish, cheese, eggs, or poultry. Try the following with French dressing:

Tossed salad of greens and fresh vegetables
Sliced tomatoes and cucumbers
Wedge of lettuce or tossed greens, such as lettuce, fresh spinach, and cabbage

The All-Important Dressing

A Spanish proverb says it takes "four persons to make a salad—a spendthrift for the oil, a miser for the vinegar, a counselor for the salt, and a madman to stir them up." Most experts don't go quite this far, but they usually agree that the kind of dressing, the amount of dressing, and the proportion of ingredients used to make the salad dressing will certainly make or break a salad. There are several basic types of dressings: French, mayonnaise, and cooked. Each has infinite variations.

Probably the most popular homemade dressing is the French type with its simple roster of basic ingredients: oil, vinegar, and seasonings. The two most important factors in making this dressing are the kinds of ingredients and proportions.

Numerous kinds of vinegars are available, any one of which can be used in salad dressings. Cider vinegar is usually considered the best. Tarragon or other herb-flavored vinegars are a little more expensive and have a distinct flavor that is not universally liked. Distilled vinegar is rather flavorless and for this reason is not recommended for dressings.

Oils vary as widely as vinegars. Olive oil is considered the gourmet's choice. But it, too, has a distinct flavor that is not always liked. So let your personal preference be your guide. The vegetable oils such as those made from corn, cottonseed or soy beans make a delicious salad and are less expensive than olive oil.

Spinach Salad

Spinach leaves, fresh and thoroughly washed
Cucumbers, chopped
1 hard-cooked egg, finely chopped
1 ounce small shrimp, precooked (optional)
1 cup mushrooms, cooked and chopped

Hand tear spinach leaves into salad bowl. Add remaining
ingredients. Mix and serve with dressing. One serving.

Calories/**150**

Garden Salad

Assorted garden lettuce (Butter and Bibb lettuce are best.)
1 medium red onion, sliced
1½ ounces sunflower seeds

Wash, drain and tear about 6 cups lettuce. Separate onion
rings. Toss ingredients.

Sour Dressing

¾ cup low-fat (2-percent) milk
¼ cup lemon juice
¼ teaspoon salt
2 tablespoons honey

Allow dressing to thicken, then toss and serve immediately.
If allowed to stand, the dressing will turn back into a thin
liquid. Serves 2.

Calories per serving/**280**

Zucchini Special

6-8 small zucchini, thinly sliced (Do not peel.)
3 ripe tomatoes, peeled and chopped
½ chopped green pepper
½ avocado, cubed
1 very small onion, grated, or 2 green onions, chopped
½ teaspoon honey
½ teaspoon salt
¼ teaspoon pepper, freshly ground

Wash zucchini thoroughly and cut into thin slices. Toss with other ingredients. Let stand for 1 hour at room temperature. Serves 6.

Calories per serving/**54**

Salad for One

Lettuce
½ cup cottage cheese
½ cup crushed pineapple (plus juice)
1 tablespoon sunflower seeds
1 slice whole grain bread, toasted, cubed

Mix all ingredients in 12-ounce bowl.

Calories/**315**

Orange and Red Onion Salad

⅓ cup sliced red onions
⅔ cup chopped lettuce and celery, mixed
1 orange, peeled and sectioned

Toss all ingredients together with fat-free Italian dressing.

Calories/**100**

Wilted Tossed Salad

3 cups fresh spinach, rinsed and torn into bite-size pieces
3 cups lettuce, rinsed and torn into bite-size pieces
½ cup sliced onion, separated into rings
8 ounces favorite cheese, grated
¼ cup shredded carrot
¼ cup chopped celery
¾ cup water
¼ cup cider vinegar
2 tablespoons sugar
1 tablespoon cornstarch
Dash pepper, salt

In large bowl, toss first 6 ingredients. In medium-size
saucepan, combine remaining ingredients. Cook and stir
until thickened. Pour hot dressing over salad; toss until
greens are coated. Serve immediately. Refrigerate leftovers.
Serves 4.

Calories per serving/**260**

Orange Cauliflower Salad

2 cans (10½ ounces each) unsweetened mandarin orange
   segments, drained
2 cups uncooked cauliflowerets
¼ cup chopped green pepper
2 cups bite-size pieces spinach
¼ cup French dressing or Orange Blossom dressing
   (See page 58.)

In large bowl, combine orange segments, cauliflowerets,
green pepper, spinach, and salad dressing. Toss and serve
immediately. Serves 4.

Calories per serving (without dressing)/**50**

Applebaum's Italiano Salad

1 small head cauliflower, separated into cauliflowerets
1 stalk broccoli, cut into flowerets
1 medium bunch celery, sliced ½-¾-inch thick
1 can whole water chestnuts, cut into quarters
1 4-ounce can whole mushrooms, sliced ¼-inch thick lengthwise
4 ounces black pitted olives, thinly sliced
3 small green onions, thinly sliced
1 pound cherry tomatoes, halved
1 small bottle low-calorie Italian dressing
Durkee Italian seasoning, to taste
Salt and pepper, to taste (not too much)

In large bowl, mix all ingredients. Marinate 24 hours. Stir
occasionally while marinating. This salad takes about
1 hour to prepare and keeps 1 week. Yield: 5 pints.
Serves 10.

Calories per serving/**74**
(½ cup)

"Being hungry isn't so tragic anymore."

Dilled Cucumbers

1 medium cucumber
1 cup buttermilk
¼ teaspoon salt (or to taste)
¼ teaspoon dill weed
⅛ teaspoon fine pepper
1 teaspoon lemon juice
1 teaspoon instant toasted onion

Remove ends and skin of cucumber; slice thinly (should yield about 1½ cups). Combine rest of ingredients in a small, deep bowl. Stir in cucumbers and chill 1 hour. *If all is eaten by 1 person, be sure to count as ½ daily milk allotment. If only the cucumber is eaten and not the excess dressing, the milk allotment is minor.*

Calories/**134**

Swedish Coleslaw

1 head cabbage
1 tablespoon salt
Water (just enough to sprinkle on layers of cabbage
    after salting)
4 stalks celery, diced
1 green pepper, diced
1 red pepper, diced

Finely shred cabbage. Place in bowl, sprinkling the layers with salt and a bit of water. Let it stand for 2 hours, then pick up by the handfuls and squeeze out the juice. Place the cabbage into another bowl and add celery, red peppers, and green peppers. Toss and add dressing.

(See following page.)

Dressing

½ cup unsweetened pineapple juice
1 cup vinegar
1 teaspoon celery seed

Combine all ingredients. Stir well, cover, and refrigerate. Stir again before serving. Serves 8.

Calories per serving/**38**

Apple Celery Salad

3 medium apples, cored
Juice of ½ lemon
2 cups diced celery
2 tablespoons chopped peanuts
1 tablespoon minced onion
½ cup low-calorie French dressing

Cut apples into small wedges and coat with lemon juice. Toss with remaining ingredients. Serve on greens. Yield: 3 cups. Serves 4.

Calories per serving/**113**

Molded Salad

1 small can frozen apple juice concentrate
2 envelopes unflavored gelatin
1 apple juice can of boiling water
1 cucumber, chopped
2 apples, diced
½ cup grated carrots

Soften gelatin in thawed apple juice concentrate. Add boiling water and stir to dissolve. Chill until partially set. Add last 3 ingredients. Continue chilling until set. Serves 6.

Calories per serving/**73**

Cottage Cheese Delight

1 8-ounce carton 2-percent fat cottage cheese
1 package low-calorie lime gelatin
1 1-pound can low-calorie fruit cocktail
½ No. 2 can crushed pineapple

In large bowl, mix all ingredients and chill. Serves 2.

Calories per serving/**265**

Chicken Salad Ah-So

2 cups diced cooked chicken
1 ½-pound can bean sprouts, drained
¼ cup sliced green onions
3 tablespoons soy sauce
2 tablespoons water
1 tablespoon sweetener
½ teaspoon ginger

In large bowl, mix all ingredients. Chill several hours or overnight. Garnish with chow mein noodles (1 tablespoon per person). Serves 4.

Calories per serving/**187**

"I eat to fuel...not to fill!"

Seafood Salad Slimmer

2 cups flaked cooked tuna or shrimp, crab or lobster
1 cup peeled, chopped cucumber
1 teaspoon salt
3 hard-cooked eggs, chopped
Salad dressing, enough for personal preference (Add calories.)

In large bowl, combine seafood, cucumber, salt, and egg. Add dressing and mix together. Salad may be chilled or served immediately. Serves 6.

Calories per serving/**145**

Tuna Salad

½ cup flaked tuna
Lemon juice, to taste
1 tablespoon OV mayonnaise*
Sweetener, to taste (optional)

Mix all ingredients together.

Calories/**183**

Citrus Cheese Salad

½ fresh grapefruit, peeled and sectioned
½ cup 2-percent-fat cottage cheese
2 tablespoons chopped cucumber
Lettuce leaf

In small bowl, combine cottage cheese and cucumber. On salad plate, arrange grapefruit on lettuce. Top with cheese mixture. Refrigerate leftovers.

Calories/**153**

*See page 52.

Hot Chicken Salad

2 cups bite-size boned chicken
   or water-packed tuna
1 cup sliced water chestnuts
2 cups diced celery
2 tablespoons OV mayonnaise*
4 ounces grated Cheddar cheese (optional; add calories)

Mix all ingredients and place in a PAM-sprayed 8-inch
Pyrex dish. Bake at 350° for 45 minutes. If grated cheese is
used, place on top for last 15 minutes. Serve with ½ cup
cooked rice (optional). Serves 6.

Calories per serving/**139**
(Add 90 calories for ½ cup rice.)

Shrimp Salad Oriental

1 16-ounce can bean sprouts, drained and rinsed
1 cup (4 ounces) cooked shrimp
½ cup chopped green onions
¼ cup thinly sliced radishes
¼ cup low-calorie Italian dressing
2 ounces mild Cheddar cheese, cubed
2 large lettuce leaves

In medium bowl, combine bean sprouts, shrimp, onions,
and radishes. Mix well. Pour dressing evenly over top.
Cover and chill 2 hours, stirring occasionally. Drain. Add
cubed cheese. Mix well. Serve on lettuce. Refrigerate leftovers. Serves 2.

Calories per serving/**252**

*See page 52.

Salad Meal

½ head cabbage, shredded
3 carrots, sliced
1 onion, chopped
1 green pepper, chopped
½ cup fresh mushrooms, sliced
6 radishes, sliced
3 medium stalks celery, cut diagonally into slices
½ cup raisins, plumped
¼ cup Caesar salad dressing

Mix vegetables with just enough dressing to moisten well. Garnish with sunflower seeds (150 calories per ounce) if desired. Serves 6.

Calories per serving/**118**

Spinach Salad

4 cups hand-torn spinach
1 cup boiling water
2 tablespoons soy sauce
1 tablespoon lemon juice
Sweetener equal to 4 teaspoons sugar

Place spinach in colander. Slowly pour boiling water over spinach. Transfer drained spinach to bowl. Combine soy sauce, lemon juice, and sweetener; pour over spinach. Toss lightly untill well mixed. Serves 4.

Calories per serving/**48**

Tomato Aspic

8 ounces tomato juice
1 envelope unflavored gelatin
½ teaspoon mixed pickling spices
1 tablespoon lemon juice
Dash pepper

Soften gelatin in tomato juice; add pickling spices. Heat to boiling. Simmer 5 minutes. Stir in lemon juice. Strain ingredients and pour into mold. Shredded vegetables, seafood, or hard-cooked eggs may be added when mixture begins to harden. Chill the aspic until firm. Unmold and serve.

Calories/**78**
(Add calories for seafood, eggs, or vegetables.)

Tomato Salad

2 medium tomatoes, sliced
¼ teaspoon onion salt
4 teaspoons wine vinegar
4 teaspoons vegetable oil
⅛ teaspoon basil leaves

Arrange tomatoes on plate. Sprinkle with onion salt, wine vinegar, vegetable oil, and basil leaves. Chill. Serves 4.

Calories per serving/**20**

Coleslaw

Chopped cabbage
Crushed pineapple (juice-packed)

Mix cabbage and pineapple. Store in tightly covered container in refrigerator.

Calories per ½ cup/**30**

"Potato" Salad

1 head cauliflowerets, cooked just until crunchy
¼ cup chopped radishes
¼ cup chopped onion
¼ cup chopped celery
¼ cup chopped green pepper
1 hard-cooked egg

In large bowl, combine all ingredients.

Dressing

4 ounces cottage cheese
3 tablespoons buttermilk
1 tablespoon prepared mustard
Sweetener, to taste
¼ cup chopped parsley
Salt and pepper, to taste

Blend dressing ingredients and mix with vegetables. Chill overnight.

Calories/**159**

Spinach Salad

3 cups trimmed fresh spinach leaves
¼ cup sliced fresh mushrooms
½ teaspoon bacon bits for each salad
½ hard-cooked egg, sliced, for each salad
Sliced tomato

Place spinach leaves in large bowl. Set aside.

Dressing

3 tablespoons lemon juice
6 tablespoons cottage cheese
3 tablespoons skim milk
¼ teaspoon instant minced onion
¼ teaspoon dill
Salt, to taste

In blender, combine all dressing ingredients. Pour over spinach leaves and divide in ½ on 2 plates. Garnish with bacon bits, egg slices, mushrooms and tomato slices. Serves 2.

Calories per serving/**126**

"To neglect God's Word is to neglect dealing with my problems His way."

Coleslaw

3 cups coarsely shredded cabbage
1 cup chopped fresh pineapple
½ cup slivered carrots, green pepper, celery,
    radishes, etc., for color
2 tablespoons low-fat Holsum Lite salad dressing
2 tablespoons milk, thin to thick-cream consistency
1 teaspoon honey if pineapple is not ripe and juicy

Remove the outer leaves and core from the cabbage. Cut off as much as is needed for use and refrigerate the remainder. Shred the cabbage and pour into a large bowl. Combine with pineapple, carrots, green pepper, celery, and radishes. Add salad dressing, milk, and honey. Toss quickly until well coated. Serve immediately. Serves 6.

Calories per serving/**42**

Pickled Fish

24 ounces cooked fish, cut into strips
3 cups water
1 cup white vinegar
2 tablespoons pickling spices
1 bay leaf
4 ounces onions, sliced
4 slices lemon
Sweetener equal to 4 tablespoons sugar

In saucepan, simmer all ingredients (except sweetener and fish) for ½ hour. Remove bay leaf after first 10 minutes. Strain the marinade; add fish and sweetener. Refrigerate 2 hours. Serves 4.

Calories per serving/**180**

Crab Salad

3½ ounces canned or fresh cooked crab meat
  or shrimp
¼ cup chopped celery
¼ cup diced cucumber and green onion
½ cup chopped salad greens and a few sliced radishes
1 apple, chopped into salad (optional)
1 tablespoon low-calorie dressing

Lightly toss all ingredients together. One serving.

Calories/**195**

Abundant Carrot Raisin Salad

Grated carrot(s) enough for 1 serving
2 tablespoons raisins or currants
3-4 tablespoons pineapple juice

Mix all ingredients together.

Calories per ½ cup/**134**

Pea Salad

1 can tiny green peas
1 cucumber, chopped
¼ cup chopped onion
Wine vinegar, to taste
2 tablespoons oil
Salt and pepper, to taste
Sweetener, to taste

Mix wine vinegar, oil, salt, pepper, and sweetener.
Marinate peas, cucumber, and onion in vinegar mixture.
Chill and serve over lettuce leaf. Serves 6.

Calories per serving/**65**

Pickled Mushrooms

2 tablespoons dehydrated onions
1 4-ounce can mushrooms, drained
½ teaspoon salt
Dash pepper
Sweetener, to taste
2 tablespoons vinegar for marinade

Combine all ingredients. Double the amount of marinade
if you use more mushrooms. Marinate a minimum of 1
hour or preferably overnight. *Suggestion: This is superb on
salads.* Use the marinade as a salad dressing. (The mushrooms add splendid flavor.)

Calories/**51**

Marinated String Beans

1 No. 2 can French-cut string beans, drained (Reserve liquid.)
1 4-ounce can sliced mushrooms, drained (Reserve liquid.)
3 tablespoons onion (flakes, minced, or green)
1 cucumber, sliced
1 ounce pimientos, drained and sliced
½ small cauliflower, cut into small pieces (optional)
¼ cup vinegar
Pepper (optional)
¼ teaspoon salt
¼ teaspoon garlic powder
¼ teaspoon seasoned salt

In large bowl, combine string beans, mushrooms, onions, cucumber, pimientos, and cauliflower. Stir in vinegar, reserved juice from beans and mushrooms, pepper (optional), salt, garlic powder, and seasoned salt. Mix thoroughly and marinate overnight. Serves 6.

Calories per serving/**26**

"I don't have to work or strive for LOVE, SELF-CONTROL, or GLADNESS—I just have to remain open to being full of Jesus."

Hot Spinach Salad

1 pound fresh spinach
¼ teaspoon salt
1 tablespoon lemon juice
¼ teaspoon Worcestershire sauce
3 tablespoons chicken bouillon
Sweetener equal to 1 teaspoon sugar

Remove stems from spinach; wash leaves and drain. Place in a large saucepan without adding any water. Cover. Steam 2-3 minutes until leaves wilt. Drain any liquid from pan. In a cup, combine lemon juice, bouillon, salt, Worcestershire sauce, and sweetener. Pour over spinach. Toss to coat leaves. Serves 4.

Calories per serving/**30**

Marinated Vegetable Medley

1 10-ounce package frozen cauliflower, thawed
1 9-ounce package frozen green beans, thawed
½ cup sliced fresh mushrooms
1 medium tomato, cut into wedges
½ cup low-calorie Italian dressing
4 ounces Colby cheese, cubed
2 medium hard-cooked eggs, quartered

Arrange vegetables in a 9-inch square Pyrex dish. Pour dressing evenly over top. Cover and chill 3 hours or overnight, stirring occasionally. To serve, drain. Arrange vegetables, cubed cheese, and eggs in salad bowl. Refrigerate leftovers. Serves 4.

Calories per serving/**219**

Cauliflower Tossed Salad

1 quart mixed salad greens, rinsed and torn
  into bite-size pieces
1 cup small fresh cauliflowerets
1 small cucumber, sliced (about ¾ cup)
1 large tomato, cut into wedges
8 ounces Cheddar cheese, cut into strips
¼ cup low-calorie sweet French-style dressing

In large salad bowl, toss greens, cauliflowerets, cucumber, and tomato. Arrange cheese strips over and among greens. Serve with dressing. Refrigerate leftovers. Serves 4.

Calories per serving/**277**

Shrimp and Mushroom Special

2 cups fresh mushrooms, thinly sliced
½ clove garlic, minced
½ cup vinegar
½ teaspoon black pepper
4 tablespoons lemon juice
1 pound cooked shrimp
1¼ teaspoons salt
Lettuce leaves

Combine mushrooms, garlic, vinegar, black pepper, and lemon juice. Marinate in refrigerator 1 hour, turning frequently. Add shrimp and salt ½ hour before serving. Serve on lettuce leaves. Serves 4.

Calories per serving/**130**

Henny Penny Salad

2 cups diced chicken
2 cups diced celery
½ small onion, chopped
½ cup grated Colby cheese
½ cup OV mayonnaise*
¼ cup sliced almonds
Bread crumbs (for garnish)

Bake all ingredients, except bread crumbs, at 350° for 30 minutes, covered. Sprinkle bread crumbs over top. Serves 6.

Calories per serving/**258**

Mini-Calorie Chicken Salad

1 cup cooked cubed chicken
½ cup diced apple, unpared
2 tablespoons chopped green pepper
2 tablespoons chopped celery
1 tablespoon finely chopped onion
2 tablespoons low-calorie Italian dressing
1 teaspoon lemon juice
4 ounces shredded or cubed Cheddar cheese
2 large lettuce leaves

In medium bowl, combine all ingredients except cheese and lettuce. Mix well. Cover and chill. Just before serving, add cheese. Serve on lettuce. Refrigerate leftovers. Yield: 2 cups. Serves 4.

Calories per serving/**218**

*See page 52.

Chef's Salad

1½ quarts mixed salad greens, rinsed and torn
   into bite-size pieces
½ cup chopped green onions
½ cup sliced radishes
¼ pound cooked chicken (white meat),
   thinly sliced and cut into strips
4 ounces Cheddar cheese, cubed
1 medium tomato, cut into wedges
1 medium hard-cooked egg, sliced
6 tablespoons low-calorie dressing

In large bowl, toss greens, onions, and radishes. Arrange
on large platter; top with remaining ingredients except
dressing. Serve with dressing. Refrigerate leftovers.
Serves 4.

Calories per serving/**241**

Tuna Toss

1½ quarts mixed salad greens, rinsed and
   torn into bite-size pieces
4 ounces Monterey Jack cheese, cut into strips
1 7-ounce can water-packed tuna, drained
1 cup (4 ounces) sliced fresh mushrooms
1 medium tomato, cut into wedges
1 small cucumber, sliced
1 medium carrot, pared and cut into 1-inch strips
5 green pepper rings
¼ cup bottled low-calorie Blue cheese dressing

Place greens in large salad bowl. Arrange remaining
ingredients except dressing over and among greens.
Cover. Chill until served. Serve with dressing. Refrigerate
leftovers. Serves 4.

Calories per serving/**199**

DIPS & DRESSINGS

Creamy Italian Dip

1 8-ounce container plain low-fat yogurt
1 12-ounce container low-fat cottage cheese
1 package Italian dressing mix

Blend all ingredients together in blender on high speed until smooth and creamy. Chill before serving.
Yield: 2½ cups.

Calories per serving/8½
(1 tablespoon)

Party Cheese Dip

1 5-ounce jar Neufchatel cheese spread with pimientos
1 cup dry cottage cheese
3 tablespoons skim milk
1 teaspoon prepared horseradish
Several drops bottled hot pepper sauce

Combine all ingredients. Beat until blended and fluffy.
Chill. *Serve with raw vegetables or as a salad dressing.*

Calories per serving/21½
(1 tablespoon)

Tomato Cheese Dip

¾ cup water
¼ cup lemon juice
1 1-pound carton low-fat cottage cheese
1 envelope dry tomato soup

Cover and blend with only ½ of cheese in blender until smooth. Add 1 envelope dry tomato soup. Mix. Cover.
Blend. Add remaining cheese and blend only until smooth.
Serve as a dip with raw, crisp, fresh vegetables.

Calories per serving/19
(1 tablespoon)

Fresh Vegetable Dip

¾ teaspoon Hidden Valley Original Mix
1 cup plain yogurt or 1 cup low-calorie cottage cheese,
    blended smooth in blender
2 teaspoons parsley
2 teaspoons dry onions or chives

If using yogurt, blend all ingredients and chill until flavors blend.

> Calories per serving/**10**
> *(1 tablespoon)*

If using cottage cheese, blend cheese in blender until smooth. Add dry ingredients and 1 teaspoon lemon juice. Chill well.

> Calories per serving/**15**
> *(1 tablespoon)*

No-Calorie French Dressing

½ cup tomato juice
½ cup vinegar
½ teaspoon dry mustard
½ tablespoon sweetener
⅛ teaspoon garlic powder
Pinch oregano, salt, and pepper

Blend all ingredients. Chill.

> Calories per serving/**¾**
> *(1 tablespoon)*

Dilly Dip

1 cup mock sour cream (page 58)
1 green onion, minced
2 tablespoons parsley
1 teaspoon dill weed

Mix all ingredients, chill and dip.

Calories per serving/**11**
(1 tablespoon)

OV* Mayonnaise

1 cup yogurt (made from skim milk)
2 tablespoons mayonnaise
¼ teaspoon salt
Dash paprika

Mix all ingredients with rotary beater until smooth.
Refrigerate 2 hours before serving.

Calories per serving/**17**
(1 tablespoon)

Zippy Tom Dressing

1 cup tomato juice
2 tablespoons lemon juice
½ small onion
½ teaspoon garlic powder (or to taste)
2 teaspoons horseradish
Dash Tabasco sauce

Mix all ingredients in blender 6-10 seconds and chill.

Calories per serving/**3**
(1 tablespoon)

*OV stands for Overeaters Victorious, a successful weight control organization based on principles from the Bible.

Salad Dressing

¼ cup vinegar
¾ cup water
Garlic powder, to taste
1 scant teaspoon celery salt
1 scant teaspoon lemon pepper
½ teaspoon sweet basil flakes
1 heaping teaspoon vegetable flakes
½-1 teaspoon Italian seasoning
Sweetener, to taste

Mix all ingredients and chill. Yield: 1 cup (16 tablespoons).

Calories per serving/**1**
(1 tablespoon)

Creamy Salad Dressing

4 ounces buttermilk
1 teaspoon vinegar
Garlic powder, to taste
1 teaspoon toasted dry onions
⅛ teaspoon salt
⅛ teaspoon finely ground black pepper

Combine buttermilk, vinegar, garlic powder, toasted dry onions, salt and pepper (in blender for best results). *Try lemon juice in place of vinegar and vary spices (tarragon, dill or salad herbs) for taste variation.*

Calories per serving/**6½**
(1 tablespoon)

Cucumber Salad Dressing

½ cup chopped cucumber
1½ teaspoon instant minced onion
1 teaspoon horseradish
½ teaspoon salt
1 cup yogurt

Beat all ingredients with rotary beater until smooth.

Calories per serving/**10**
(1 tablespoon)

Curry-Caper Salad Dressing

1 cup yogurt
¼ cup mayonnaise
¼ teaspoon salt
¼ teaspoon curry powder
⅛ teaspoon garlic powder
½ teaspoon instant beef bouillon
2 tablespoons capers, drained

Blend all ingredients until smooth.

Calories per serving/**20**
(1 tablespoon)

*"Constant comfort tends to dull me...
but DISCIPLINE sharpens my character."*

Bonanza Dressing

1 cup buttermilk
1 tablespoon dehydrated onion flakes
Dash paprika
½ teaspoon onion bouillon powder
Dash onion powder
1 tablespoon dried chives
Dash salt
A shake of garlic and/or dill weed may be added.

In a jar, mix all ingredients thoroughly. Put into refrigerator
1 hour before serving. *Great as a dressing on salad.*
Especially tasty mixed with tuna. To use as a dip, add ½ packet
unflavored gelatin to thicken.

Calories per serving/6¼
(1 tablespoon) Add 1 calorie
for each tablespoon of unflavored
gelatin.

Blue Cheese Dressing

½ teaspoon gelatin
1 tablespoon vinegar
1 tablespoon water
1 teaspoon powdered chicken bouillon
1 cup buttermilk
¼ teaspoon onion salt
¼ teaspoon garlic powder
1 ounce Blue cheese (Note cheese allotment.)

Heat water and vinegar. Dissolve gelatin and bouillon.
Let mixture cool. Crumble cheese and add to first
mixture. Add seasoning. Add buttermilk and stir. Chill
and serve.

Calories per serving/9
(1 tablespoon)

Salad Dressing

1 tablespoon safflower oil
½ cup white vinegar
½ cup water
Paprika (for color)
Dehydrated onion and dry mustard, to taste
Pinch powdered tarragon leaves

Mix all ingredients in 8-ounce dressing bottle. *For variation add Tabasco for hot taste or any sweetener for sweet/sour taste.*

Calories per serving/**9**
(1 tablespoon)

Blue Cheese Dressing

1 cup cream-style cottage cheese
⅓ cup water
2 tablespoons crumbled Blue cheese
1 teaspoon Worcestershire sauce

Blend all ingredients until smooth. Chill. Yield: 1 cup.

Calories per serving/**18**
(1 tablespoon)

Mayonnaise Slender

1 egg
1 cup safflower oil
¼ teaspoon dry mustard
2 tablespoons lemon juice or vinegar
Salt, to taste

Blend ¼ cup of the oil with the other ingredients for 10 seconds. Slowly pour in remaining oil until blended. *May be used in chicken or seafood salads.*

Calories per serving/**30**
(1 tablespoon)

Italian Dressing

1 tablespoon safflower oil
½ tablespoon white vinegar
½ tablespoon water
1 teaspoon Grey Poupon mustard
Oregano, garlic powder, and pepper, to taste

Mix all ingredients and shake well. *Triple, or make as much as you like!* Keep refrigerated.

Calories per serving/**75**
(1 tablespoon)

Buttermilk Dressing

1 cup buttermilk
½ cup OV Mayonnaise*
¼ cup sweet pickle relish
1 tablespoon prepared mustard
1 teaspoon salt
¼ teaspoon garlic powder
¼ teaspoon dill weed
⅛ teaspoon pepper
2 tablespoons chopped parsley

In bowl, mix buttermilk, mayonnaise, relish, and mustard. Blend in remaining ingredients. Yield: 2 cups.

Calories per serving/**19**
(1 tablespoon)

*See page 52.

Mock Sour Cream

1 8-ounce carton low-fat (2-percent) cottage cheese
2 tablespoons skim milk
1 teaspoon lemon juice

Blend all ingredients until smooth and creamy. *Use as a sour cream substitute. Good on salads or as a dip.*

Calories per serving/**13**
(1 tablespoon)

Orange Blossom Dressing

1 13-ounce can evaporated skim milk
1 6-ounce can frozen orange juice concentrate, thawed

Shake ingredients together in jar. Refrigerate.

Calories per serving/**20**
(1 tablespoon)

"Try to please Him...just until noon!"

SOUPS & SAUCES

Velvet Cheese Soup

1 cup skim milk
4 ounces Cheddar cheese, grated
1½ cups water
1 packet instant chicken broth and seasoning mix or
  1 chicken bouillon cube
1 packet instant beef broth and seasoning mix or
  2 beef bouillon cubes
1 cup (8-ounce package) frozen chopped broccoli, thawed
2 tablespoons diced pimientos
1 tablespoon dehydrated onion flakes
½ teaspoon butter flavoring
Salt and pepper, to taste

Combine milk and cheese in a saucepan. Stir over low heat
until cheese begins to melt. Add water and broth mixes.
Stir until cheese is completely melted. Add remaining
ingredients. Cook over low heat 5 minutes longer, stirring
frequently, until broccoli is tender. Divide evenly.
Serves 2 (luncheon).

Calories per serving/**323**

---

*"GOD KNOWS ME! He remembers how weak
I am even when He tells me to be strong!"*

Vegetable Tomato Soup

1 48-ounce can tomato juice or V-8 juice
1 tablespoon instant beef bouillon
1 20-ounce package frozen mixed vegetables or
   to thicken the above stock, use shredded or chopped seasonal
   vegetables such as cabbage, cauliflower, carrots, rutabaga,
   onion, green pepper (careful), mushrooms, tomato (lots),
   celery, turnips

Do not use high-calorie vegetables. Omit potato. Add leftover rice casserole if desired. Bring juice and bouillon to boil. Add vegetables in order of the length of time needed to cook through. Simmer. Adjust seasoning (garlic is good). Length of time to cook depends on how large a pot is used. Serves 10.

Calories per serving/**54**

Golden-Light Side Soup

2 tablespoons chopped celery
2 tablespoons chopped onion
1 tablespoon margarine
2 tablespoons unsifted flour
2 cups skim milk
½ teaspoon dry mustard
½ teaspoon salt
¼ teaspoon paprika
1 cup grated Cheddar cheese

In medium saucepan, cook celery and onion in margarine; stir in flour. Add milk, mustard, salt, and paprika. Cook and stir over medium heat until thickened. Add cheese product. Cook and stir until cheese melts. Serve immediately. Refrigerate leftovers. Serves 4.

Calories per serving/**276**

Vichyssoise

3 envelopes or cubes chicken broth
3 cups water
1 medium-head cauliflower, separated into ½-inch flowerets
¼ cup instant minced onion flakes
2 sprigs parsley
1 stalk celery, sliced
3 drops Worcestershire sauce
1 teaspoon butter
⅛ teaspoon nutmeg
1 cup skim milk
4 teaspoons chives (for garnish)

Combine bouillon and water in saucepan; bring to a boil.
Add cauliflower, onion flakes, parsley, celery, and Worcestershire sauce. Simmer 10 minutes or until celery is tender.
Stir in butter and nutmeg. Let stand at room temperature
30 minutes. Transfer to blender; run at medium speed for 4
minutes or until vegetables are pureed, or put through a
very fine sieve. Stir in milk. Chill in refrigerator for at least
2 hours. Before serving, sprinkle each portion with 1
teaspoon chives. Serves 4.

Calories per serving/**81**

Tomato Soup

1 6-ounce can tomato juice
Cumin, chili powder, or oregano, to taste
1 tablespoon vinegar
Sweetener, to taste
1 4-ounce can tomatoes, pureed

Simmer all ingredients until heated through.

Calories/**62**

Broccoli and Chicken Soup

2 halves or 1 whole chicken breast, skinned
7 cups water
3 cups chopped broccoli
1 cup chopped celery
1 cup chopped green onion
5 teaspoons chicken bouillon
¼ teaspoon garlic powder
½ teaspoon onion powder
1 teaspoon seasoned salt

Boil chicken in water until thoroughly cooked. Take chicken
from water, remove bones, and weigh out 6 ounces. Dice
and put back into 6 cups of broth in which the chicken was
boiled. If not enough broth, extend with water. Add
the broccoli, celery, green onion, chicken bouillon, garlic
powder, onion powder, and seasoned salt. Simmer 30-45
minutes. Yield: 7 cups.

Calories per serving/**57**
(1 cup)

Broccoli and Chicken Soup, *Simplified Version*

1 10½-ounce can chicken broth
1 cup water
2 5-ounce cans chicken
1 package frozen chopped broccoli
3 stalks celery, chopped
4 green onions, chopped
Garlic, onion powder, and seasoned salt, to taste

In a saucepan, combine all ingredients except the chicken.
Cook until vegetables are tender. Add chicken and cook
until it is heated through. Serves 4.

Calories per serving/**95**

Vegetable Veal Soup

½ pound ground veal
1 1-pound can tomatoes
1 8-ounce can tomato sauce (optional)
1 12-ounce can V-8 juice
2 cups water
1 10-ounce package frozen mixed vegetables
¼ cup dry onion soup mix

Brown veal, drain off fat and blot excess fat with paper towels. Stir veal into remaining ingredients. Bring to boil, then simmer 20 minutes. Serves 6-8.

Calories per serving/**162**
(6 servings)

Broccoli Cheese Soup

2 tablespoons margarine or butter
3 tablespoons flour
⅓-½ onion, minced
1½ cups boiling water
1-2 bouillon cubes
1 cup steamed broccoli
1 cup (3 ounces) shredded American cheese

Make white sauce by combining margarine, flour, water, and bouillon. Add broccoli and cheese. Spice to taste.
Excellent and filling meal.

Calories per serving/**250**
(1 cup)

Cream of Mushroom Soup

1 small can or jar mushroom pieces (Save liquid.)
1 cup liquid nonfat milk
1 cube or envelope beef bouillon
Salt and pepper, to taste

Blend mushrooms and ½ mushroom juice, bouillon, and milk in a blender. Do not blend the mushrooms too finely. Add salt and pepper. Heat and serve.

Calories/**118**

Gazpacho (Basic)

2 medium cucumbers, chopped
1 quart tomato juice
2 cloves garlic, minced
2 tablespoons vinegar
2 teaspoons salt
1 teaspoon ground cumin
4 ice cubes
Green pepper, diced (optional, for garnish)
1 slice toast, crumbled (optional)
2 ounces fresh onion (optional)
2 ounces chopped tomato (optional)

In a bowl, combine cucumbers and tomato juice; let mixture soak 1 hour. Blend at high speed in a blender. Strain into a large mixing bowl. Add garlic, vinegar, salt, cumin, and ice cubes. Chill. To serve, sprinkle diced green pepper and diced cucumber over soup. For lunch, add bread crumbs. For dinner, add chopped tomato and fresh onion. Serves 6.

Calories:
For basic serving/**36**
For lunch serving/**101**
For dinner serving/**105**

"Free" Soup

½ head lettuce, chopped
½ head cabbage, chopped
1 medium onion, chopped
1 medium bell pepper, chopped
3 stalks celery, diced
1 16-ounce can tomatoes (plus juice)
1 16-ounce can tomato sauce
Water to cover

Place in large (4-6 quart) pot and cook 3-4 hours over medium heat. Serves 10.

Calories per serving/**43**

Cabbage Soup

1 46-ounce can tomato juice
7 tablespoons lemon juice
2 tablespoons dehydrated onions
½ cup water
2 envelopes powdered beef bouillon
Sweetener, to taste
½ medium-head cabbage, shredded

In a saucepan, combine all ingredients except cabbage; bring to a boil over medium heat. Add cabbage. Serves 8.

Calories per serving/**48**

Mock Split Pea Soup

3 cups water
1 envelope onion bouillon
6 stalks celery, diced
1 1-pound can string beans
6 sprigs parsley
1 pound asparagus pieces, cooked
⅛ teaspoon mace
1 bay leaf
Salt and pepper, to taste

In blender, combine all ingredients except seasonings.
Blend at high speed. Pour mixture into soup kettle. Add
seasonings. Simmer for ½ hour or more. Discard bay leaf
and serve hot. Serves 4.

Calories per serving/**159**

Tangy Tomato Broth

1 cup beef bouillon
1 cup tomato juice
Parsley (dry flakes)

Combine beef bouillon and tomato juice. Heat. Pour into
cups. Sprinkle with parsley. Serve piping hot. Serves 4.

Calories per serving/**14**
(½ cup)

Marinara Sauce

1 4-ounce can tomato juice
2 teaspoons onion powder or flakes
Small amount garlic powder
3 green peppers, cut into large chunks
2 teaspoons basil
1 16-ounce can mushrooms, drained
½ teaspoon oregano

In medium pan, combine tomato juice, onion, garlic, peppers, and basil. Cook 45 minutes. Stir in mushrooms during the last 10 minutes. Add oregano within the last 5 minutes *only*. (If added sooner, it will become bitter.)

This sauce may be refrigerated 1-2 weeks and is great over green peas, French-cut string beans, leftover fish, chicken or veal. (When using leftovers, be sure to measure out the proper caloric allowances.) *The combination makes a delicious and complete meal.*

Calories per serving/**25**
(½ cup)

Seafood Cocktail Sauce

¾ cup boiled-down tomato juice (1 cup before boiling)
2 tablespoons Worcestershire sauce
1 teaspoon (or less) horseradish
1½ teaspoons lemon juice
½ teaspoon seasoned salt
1 teaspoon onion powder

Place all ingredients in a jar with a tight-fitting lid. Shake well.

Calories per tablespoon/**33**

BBQ Sauce

1 cup V-8 juice or tomato juice
⅓ cup vinegar
2 tablespoons cornstarch
2 teaspoons Worcestershire sauce
¼ teaspoon garlic powder
¼ teaspoon chili powder

In a saucepan, stir all ingredients. Cook over medium heat until thickened, then cook 3-5 minutes longer to blend flavors. *Try this sauce on barbecued chicken, hamburgers, steaks, etc.* Yield: 1⅓ cups.

Calories per tablespoon/**6**

Cucumber Dill Sauce

1 medium cucumber, shredded to make 1 cup
½ cup plain yogurt
¼ cup mayonnaise
1 tablespoon snipped parsley
1 teaspoon lemon juice
2 teaspoons grated onion
½ teaspoon dried dill weed
¼ teaspoon salt
Dash pepper

Combine all ingredients. Blend well and chill. Garnish with cucumber twist. *Good with fish.* Yield: 1½ cups.

Calories per serving/**25**
(3 *tablespoons*)

Mushroom Sauce

1 cup beef-flavor broth or
  1 beef bouillon cube in 1 cup water
8 ounces fresh mushrooms, sliced (about 2½ cups)
3 green onions, minced
1 tablespoon flour mixed with 3 tablespoons water

In a large skillet, bring the broth to a boil. Add mushrooms
and green onions. Reduce heat to medium-low; cover and
cook 6 minutes. Strain out the mushrooms and onions; set
aside. Stir in the flour/water mixture. Cook and stir until
the sauce thickens. Return the mushrooms and onions to
the mixture. Simmer 2 minutes.

Calories per serving/**28**
(¼ cup)

*"God has begun a good work—He will continue
with me...I must continue with Him."*

ENTREES
BREAKFAST, LUNCH OR DINNER

If the Price of Meat Is Butchering Your Budget

Try Grain Supplements

This chart shows how to get all the amino acids we need to produce protein—by combining foods that will supply us with the essential eight amino acids. (It takes 22 different amino acids to make protein. Fourteen are produced by our bodies, eight are obtained from the food we eat. If one is missing, no protein is produced.) The grains at the top (whole-wheat flour, white flour, rice, and oatmeal) when combined with buttermilk OR cream cheese OR cottage cheese OR one of the rest of the foods listed will produce the amount of protein indicated under the grain listing. For example, one cup of whole-wheat flour and ½ cup of buttermilk will produce 16 grams of protein—more than you'll get in a lamb chop. It all goes to prove that you can eliminate meat from your diet and still get the necessary protein that your body requires.

	one cup WHOLE WHEAT FLOUR	one cup WHITE FLOUR	one cup UNCOOKED RICE	one cup UNCOOKED OATMEAL
protein potential	16 gms	11.6 gms ...	14.5 gms ...	11.4 gms ...
Eggs	2	2	1	1 ....
Buttermilk	½ cup	¾ cup	¼ cup	⅓ cup ......
Cream Cheese .	2 Tbsp	3 Tbsp	2 Tbsp	3 Tbsp .....
Cottage Cheese	2 Tbsp	4 Tbsp	2 Tbsp	3 Tbsp .....
Gelatin	½ Tbsp	1 Tbsp	¼ Tbsp	½ Tbsp .....
Corn	1½ cups	1½ cups	½ cup	½ cup ......
Cornmeal	1 cup	1 cup	¼ cup	½ cup ......
Garbanzo Beans	¼ cup	1 cup	¼ cup	¾ cup ......
Baker's Yeast ...	2 Tbsp	not enough sulphurs		3 Tbsp .....
Brewer's Yeast	2 Tbsp	not enough sulphurs		
Lima Beans	¼ cup			
Green Peas	⅔ cup			
Dry Milk	3 Tbsp			
Peanut Butter ..	8 Tbsp			
Wheat Germ ...	½ cup			
Cheddar Cheese	1 oz			
Soybean Flour ..	2 Tbsp			
Coconut				¾ cup .....

What It Costs to Buy
a Day's Worth of Protein *December 1981*

Item	Cost for 44 grams*
Dry, Split Peas	$0.14
Dry, White Northern Beans	0.22
Jack Mackerel	0.35
Turkey	0.40
Broiler-Fryers	0.44
Blade Pot Roast	0.48
Shank Ham	0.53
Eggs	0.53
Ground Beef (70% lean)	0.75
Hot Dogs	0.75
Peanut Butter	0.79
Cottage Cheese	0.84
Pork Loin Roast	0.84
Tuna	0.92
Sardines	0.97
Round Steak	1.01
Muenster Cheese	1.10
Canned Pork and Beans	1.18
Spareribs	1.58
Yogurt	2.77

*The recommended daily allowance for adult women.

Pancakes

1 slice whole grain bread, toasted, crumbled in blender
1 egg
⅛ teaspoon baking powder
⅛ teaspoon vanilla
1 teaspoon sweetener
1 ounce orange juice (or use 2 tablespoons water
   to reduce calories)

In blender, combine bread crumbs, egg, baking powder,
vanilla, sweetener, and orange juice (or water). Blend.
Drop by spoonfuls into a hot non-stick fry pan. Turn over
when bubbles begin to burst. Yield: 6 pancakes.

Calories per pancake/**27**

Hash-Brown Casserole

24 ounces shredded raw potatoes
   or thawed hash browns
1 medium onion, chopped
1 4-ounce can mushrooms, drained
1 can cream-of-mushroom soup
1½ cups shredded Cheddar cheese
⅛ cup wheat germ
Salt and pepper, to taste

Bake all ingredients at 350° for 1 hour or until golden
brown. Serves 4-6 adults.

Calories per 2 cups/**200**

Spanish Omelet

1 egg, well-beaten
1 ounce Monterey Jack cheese, shredded
1 tablespoon chopped Ortega chilies
Salsa

Spray fry pan with PAM. Pour beaten egg into pan. Cook until set. On top of egg place cheese and chilies. Fold ½ of egg over onto the other ½. Cover and cook until cheese melts. Top with salsa. If desired, heat salsa first in small pan. Serve with freshly sliced tomatoes, carrot and celery sticks, or green salad. One serving.

Calories/**191**

Breakfast Delight Omelet

1 ounce ground round steak
1 egg
Salt and pepper, to taste
Pinch of dry mustard
Tabasco sauce (optional)

Hand crumble ground round steak in Teflon pan. Cook until brown. Remove from pan onto paper towel. In separate bowl, mix egg, salt, pepper, dry mustard, and Tabasco sauce (optional). Pour into pan and mix with the meat. Cook until set. Fold ½ of omelet over onto the other ½. One serving.

Calories/**130**

Sour Cream Scrambled Eggs

4 eggs
4 tablespoons sour cream
2 green onions, sliced into thin rings
¼ teaspoon tarragon
Dash salt and pepper
Fresh mushrooms, heated and sauteed
   in PAM-sprayed pan

In a bowl, combine eggs and other ingredients; beat with a
fork. Heat a 10-inch PAM-sprayed pan. Pour in the egg
mixture and reduce the heat. Scramble gently until set.
Serve with sauteed mushrooms. Serves 4.

Calories per serving/**116**

Apple Danish

½ large green or red apple
1 ounce Monterey Jack cheese
1 slice bread
Cinnamon, to taste

Toast bread and warm apple (place in microwave on
"high" for 1 minute or place in steamer for 2 minutes).
Slice apple and place on toast. Cover with cheese and
sprinkle with cinnamon. Place under broiler until cheese
melts or in microwave on "high" for 45 seconds. *Delectable.*
One serving.

Calories/**200**

Fruit Fritter

½ apple, shredded
   or ½ banana, sliced
   or ½ peach, coarsely diced
   or 1 apricot, coarsely diced
   or ½ cup berries
1 slice bread
1 egg, beaten
2 tablespoons nonfat milk
⅛ teaspoon butter flavoring (optional)
Cinnamon, to taste

Tear bread into bite-size pieces and mix with other ingredients. Pour into a PAM-sprayed skillet and cook until brown on both sides. One serving.

Calories:

Apple Fritter/**183**
Banana Fritter/**199**
Peach Fritter/**175**
Apricot Fritter/**173**
Berry Fritter/**196**

---

*"Face God with the problem,
and then face the problem with God."*

French Toast

1 egg
3 tablespoons skim milk
½ teaspoon vanilla
Dash salt
¼ teaspoon cinnamon
1 slice bread
Sweetener, to taste

Combine egg, skim milk, vanilla, salt, and sweetener. Dip bread in egg mixture until it absorbs the mixture. Place the bread on a hot griddle or in a fry pan. Pour remaining egg mixture over the bread. Brown each side of the bread. One serving.

Calories/**169**

Blueberry Cheese Danish

⅓ cup Ricotta or cottage cheese
½ cup blueberries
½ teaspoon vanilla or almond flavoring
Cinnamon, to taste
Sweetener, to taste
1 slice bread, toasted

Combine cheese, blueberries, flavoring, cinnamon, and sweetener. Spread on toast and place under broiler until heated through. One serving.

Calories/**200**

Banana Danish

1 banana, sliced
¼ cup Ricotta or cottage cheese
¼ teaspoon vanilla or banana flavoring
Sweetener, to taste
1 slice bread, toasted

In a bowl, mash ½ banana slices. Add the cheese, vanilla, and sweetener to banana; mix. Spread ½ cheese mixture on toast and top with banana slices. Spread remaining cheese mixture over the banana slices. Broil until lightly browned. One serving.

Calories/**254**

Mud Omelet

2 eggs, lightly beaten
1-2 teaspoons cinnamon
1-2 packets sugar substitute
¼ cup cottage cheese

Mix all ingredients. Cook in skillet with margarine or PAM. *Enjoy!* One serving.

Calories/**209**

Cottage Cheese Pancakes

6 eggs
¼ teaspoon salt
¼ cup flour
1 cup cottage cheese

In blender, blend eggs and salt until smooth. Add flour; blend. With blender running, add cottage cheese until mixed in (do not mix smooth). *Note:* If preparing in mixer, mix cottage cheese first, then salt and eggs, then flour. For toppings, use honey, butter, fruit, syrup (count calories), or peel and slice a peach. Place in small saucepan with ½ cup water. Add cinnamon and sweetener or honey. Cook until peace slices appear translucent or soft. Pour over pancakes. Serves 6.

Calories per serving/**108**
(3 4-inch pancakes)

"SACRIFICE leads to legalism—
OBEDIENCE leads to liberty—
The difference is on the INSIDE."

Pizza Sauce

16 ounces tomato sauce
1 teaspoon garlic powder
1 tablespoon oregano leaves
1 tablespoon basil leaves
Sweetener equal to 2 teaspoons sugar
Salt and pepper, to taste

Combine all ingredients. Simmer over low heat until thickened. One serving.

Calories/**50**
(½ cup)

Pizza Sandwiches (Open-Faced)

2 slices bread, extra-thin
2 ounces Farmer's cheese*, thinly sliced
2 4-ounce cans mushrooms, drained
Ground oregano, to taste
Pizza sauce (See recipe above.)

Toast bread. Divide mushrooms and place on toast. Cover with pizza sauce (1-1½ tablespoons is plenty per slice). Place cheese on top and sprinkle with oregano. Place under broiler until cheese melts and browns lightly. One serving.

Calories/**177**
(including 3 tablespoons pizza sauce)

---

*Other cheeses may be used, but you will have to adjust the calorie count. Farmer's cheese can be found at Hickory Farms and is only 40 calories per ounce.

"Pizza"

1 slice bread, toasted
1 ounce Cheddar, Mozzarella,
   or Monterey Jack cheese
Catsup, small amount
Oregano, to taste

Spread catsup on bread. Add cheese and oregano. Broil until cheese is bubbly. *Very good!* One serving.

Calories/**175**

Veal Pizza

Veal choppies*, a sufficient number
   to feed your family
Chopped mushrooms, black olives,
   or other favorite pizza toppings
Grated Mozzarella cheese

Broil veal choppies 2½ minutes on each side. Remove meat from broiler and place in a single layer in a jelly roll pan. Cover with tomato sauce and other pizza toppings. Sprinkle with Mozzarella cheese and bake at 400° until cheese melts.

Tomato Sauce

1 16-ounce can tomato sauce with tomato bits
1 small onion, finely chopped
2 teaspoons Italian seasoning
1 teaspoon oregano

Combine tomato sauce ingredients and let stand 15 minutes to season. Serves 6.

Calories per serving/**177**
(Add 50 calories per tomato sauce serving.)

---

*Four ounces of veal equal 127 calories. Veal choppies weigh light because they are made from whatever is left on the bone after the regular cuts have been taken. The meat is ground like hamburger and formed into patties.

Turkey/Squash Bake

½ acorn squash
3 ounces ground turkey
1 teaspoon chopped onion
1 teaspoon chopped celery
1 teaspoon chopped mushrooms
1 tablespoon butter or margarine
2 tablespoons milk
Paprika, to taste
Sage and/or poultry seasoning (optional)

Cut squash in ½; scoop out seeds. Place ½ squash upside-down on baking tray; sauté with butter or margarine (to cut calories, substitute butter salt and broth). Bake until tender, about 45 minutes at 350°. While the squash is baking, brown the ground turkey in skillet (if leftover, grind first). Add the chopped onion, celery, and mushrooms; mix together.

When the squash is baked, scoop it out of the shell, mash; combine with the turkey mixture and milk. Whip the turkey/squash mixture until fluffy and return it to the squash shell. Sprinkle with paprika, sage and/or poultry seasoning. Return to oven 15-20 minutes until slightly crusty. One serving.

Calories/**335**

Diane's Delight

1 pound lean ground beef
1-2 green onions, chopped
1 cup celery, diagonally sliced
1 can water chestnuts, sliced
1 green pepper, cut into bite-size pieces
Salt and pepper, to taste
1-2 tablespoons soy sauce
1 pound fresh bean sprouts (or 1 can, but fresh bean
    sprouts taste better)

Brown the meat until crumbly. Drain excess fat. Add
onions, celery, green pepper, water chestnuts, salt,
pepper, and soy sauce. Simmer until vegetables are cooked.

Meanwhile, cook the bean sprouts in salted water until
tender. Drain. Add to meat mixture. Mix thoroughly and
simmer another 5-10 minutes. Serve with cooked rice
(optional). Serves 4-6.

Calories per serving:
Recipe divided into 4/**236**
Recipe divided into 6/**157**
*(Add 90 calories per ½ cup rice,
if served.)*

*"I give my body what it requires...
not what it desires!"*

Spinach Meat Loaf

1 pound lean ground beef
1 package (10 ounces) frozen chopped spinach,
   thawed and drained
1 egg, lightly beaten
⅔ cup seasoned dressing mix or seasoned bread crumbs
¼ teaspoon pepper
⅛ teaspoon garlic powder
1 can mushroom sauce

Mix all ingredients thoroughly. Put into an ungreased loaf
pan (5 inches by 9 inches). Bake in 350° oven 60 minutes
or microwave on medium setting 20 minutes. Let stand 5
minutes. Heat the mushroom sauce and pour it over the
meat loaf. Serves 6.

Calories per serving/**176**

Slim Jim Chili

1 pound lean ground beef
½ cup chopped onion
2 cups sliced celery (optional)
½ cup chopped green pepper
½ teaspoon garlic salt
1 15-ounce can (1¾ cups) kidney beans, undrained
2 1-pound cans (4 cups) tomatoes, undrained
1-2 teaspoons salt
½-1 tablespoon chili powder
1 bay leaf

Brown meat and onion in Dutch oven or large fry pan;
thoroughly drain all excess fat. Add remaining ingredients.
Simmer, uncovered, 1-2 hours. Remove bay leaf. Serve
hot. Serves 8.

Calories per serving/**156**
(1 cup)

Hurry Beef Stew

4 medium carrots (2 cups), cut into 1½-inch pieces
4 medium stalks celery (2 cups), cut into 1½-inch pieces
½ pound lean beef, cubed and cooked
1½ cups water
1 cup tomato juice
2 small turnips, quartered
1 medium onion, quartered
1 teaspoon salt
½ teaspoon garlic salt or ¼ teaspoon instant
   minced garlic
¼ teaspoon pepper
1 bay leaf
1 beef bouillon cube or 1 teaspoon instant
   beef bouillon

In large saucepan, combine all ingredients. Bring to a boil.
Reduce heat; simmer, covered, 45-60 minutes until vegetables are tender and flavors well-blended. Remove bay
leaf. To thicken juices, combine 2 tablespoons flour with ¼
cup cold water; mix thoroughly. Drizzle over stew and stir
very gently until sauce thickens. Serves 4.

Calories per serving/**171**
(1⅓ cups)

*"Today I may not be doing very well...
but I am doing better than yesterday."*

Pot Pie

6 ounces turkey, chicken, or beef,
  cubed and cooked
½ onion, chopped
1 package frozen chopped broccoli, partially thawed
1 tomato, finely chopped
1 stalk celery, finely chopped
1 carrot, finely chopped
2 chicken or beef bouillon cubes, dissolved
  in ½ cup water
¼ teaspoon sage
Dash garlic powder and pepper
1 potato, peeled and cubed
1 teaspoon diet margarine
1 tablespoon nonfat milk
2 tablespoons Parmesan cheese
Paprika, to taste

Put first 10 ingredients into a Pyrex 1½-quart casserole
dish. Mix and smooth mixture until top is flat. In a saucepan, boil the potato until tender; drain liquid and mash.
Add diet margarine, milk, and cheese; mix thoroughly.
Spread mixture on top of casserole. Sprinkle with paprika.
Place in 375° oven for 30 minutes. (Do not cover the dish;
the top of the pot pie should be browned. To further brown
the top, place pie under broiler.) Serves 4.

Calories per serving:
Turkey/**139**
Chicken/**129**
Hamburger/**153**
Roast or Round Steak/**137**

Stuffed Bell Peppers

2 large bell peppers
⅔ cup cooked rice
6 ounces hamburger
1 4-ounce can mushrooms, drained
1 stalk celery, finely chopped
1 large tomato, finely chopped
1 tablespoon Worcestershire sauce
⅓ cup water

Wash, half and clean out insides of bell peppers. Place cut side up, in an 8-inch by 10-inch pan. Brown hamburger, drain well. Add other ingredients, except water, and stir. Spoon equally into pepper shells. Pour water into pan and cover with foil (Saran Wrap for microwave). Bake in oven at 350° for 45 minutes or microwave on medium setting for 23 minutes. Let stand, covered, 5 minutes before serving. Serves 4 (or 2, if you're hungry!).

Calories per serving/**161**
(Double serving/322)

Chicken Cacciatore

4 chicken breasts, skinned
2 small green peppers, chopped
1 clove garlic, minced
2 tablespoons chopped pimientos
1 bay leaf
⅛ teaspoon thyme
1 tablespoon dried parsley
1 cup mushrooms, chopped
2 cups stewed tomatoes

Combine all ingredients; simmer 45 minutes. Serve over cooked rice. Serves 4.

Calories per serving/**159**
(Add 76 calories per ½ cup rice.)

Chicken Salad Slenderizer

3 cups cubed or flaked cooked chicken
1½ cups peeled and diced cucumber
3 hard-cooked eggs, chopped
1 teaspoon salt substitute
Salad dressing (See below.)

In bowl, mix chicken, cucumber, egg, and salt substitute.
Combine with desired amount of salad dressing. The salad
may be chilled before serving or eaten immediately.
Serves 4.

Salad Dressing

1 tablespoon safflower oil
½ cup white vinegar
½ cup water
Paprika, to taste
Onion flakes, to taste
Pinch tarragon
¾ teaspoon prepared mustard

In jar or bottle, combine salad dressing ingredients
and shake. Chill.

Calories per serving/**313**

"*Focus on the salvation WITHIN and get it out!*"

Heavenly Chicken

2 tablespoons chives
¼ cup chopped fresh parsley
½ pound fresh mushrooms, sliced
4 chicken breasts
½ cup lemon juice
1 teaspoon paprika
½ teaspoon salt
½ teaspoon poultry seasoning

Mix chives, parsley, and mushrooms; put them into a plastic baking bag. Place the chicken on the mushrooms; pour lemon juice over it, then sprinkle with onion powder, paprika, and poultry seasoning. Place the bag of chicken and seasonings into a baking dish; cover, and bake at 325° for about 35 minutes, until chicken is done. If more juice is desire, add ½ cup water. Serves 4.

Calories per serving/**333**

Baked Chicken

1 4-ounce chicken breast with bone
1 4-ounce chicken thigh with bone
½ cup buttermilk (1-percent fat)
¼ cup lemon juice
Seasoning, to taste

Preheat oven to 350°. Place chicken parts in shallow pan. Mix other ingredients and pour over chicken. Cover the pan and bake at 350° for 45-60 minutes. Serves 2.

Calories per serving/**135**

Chicken Milan

10½ ounces chicken breasts
1 cup chopped celery
2 tablespoons chopped parsley
1 small bay leaf
⅛ teaspoon thyme
½ cup tomatoes
1¼ cups mushrooms, quartered
1 cup water or de-fatted broth
Salt and pepper, to taste

Brown chicken in Teflon pan glazed with diet dressing, then transfer to casserole with cover. Add celery, parsley, bay, thyme, tomatoes, and broth or water. Cover and bake at 350° for 45 minutes; add mushrooms and cook 15 minutes longer or until chicken is tender. Remove bay leaf, add salt and pepper, sprinkle chopped parsley on top, and serve from casserole. Serves 3.

Calories per serving/**118**

Lemon Baked Chicken

2 ½-pound chicken breasts
2 teaspoons butter or margarine
½ teaspoon salt
¼ teaspoon paprika
Lemon juice
Parsley, snipped

Preheat oven to 425°. Remove skin from chicken. Split breasts. Place chicken in ungreased baking pan. Spread 1 teaspoon soft butter or margarine on the chicken pieces. Sprinkle with salt and paprika. Drizzle with lemon juice. Bake, uncovered, for 35-45 minutes, until tender. Sprinkle with snipped parsley. Serves 2.

Calories per serving/**225**

Barbecued Baked Chicken

1 2½-pound chicken

Preheat oven to 350°. Disjoint the chicken and place in a
shallow baking pan. Baste with the barbecue sauce (see
below). Bake uncovered 30-40 minutes, until tender,
basting with the barbecue sauce and turning occasionally.
Serves 2.

Barbecue Sauce

1 cup tomato juice
Diced celery, to taste
Onion bits, to taste
Dash vinegar
Dry mustard, to taste
Pinch sugar

Combine all ingredients.

Calories per serving/**60**

Hickory Baked Chicken

1 2½-pound chicken
Hickory smoked salt

Preheat oven to 400°. Sprinkle whole chicken generously
with hickory smoked salt. Place on roasting rack in oven
and bake 1 hour. Turn and bake back side for another 30
minutes. Serves 2.

Calories per serving/**60**

Chicken Salad Hawaiian

1 16-ounce can chunk-style pineapple (juice-packed)
1½ cups cubed cooked chicken
1 cup chopped celery
1 cup halved green grapes
   (Thompson seedless, if possible)
½ cup chopped walnuts
Salt, to taste
¼ cup thawed orange juice concentrate

Combine all ingredients and toss. Serves 3.

Calories per serving/**386**

Chicken Enchiladas

16 corn tortillas
16 ounces chicken breasts, skinned
8 ounces Cheddar, Monterey Jack, Farmer's,
   or Mozzarella cheese
4 cups sauce (See following page.)
2½ ounces cheese (for garnish)
3½ ounces green chilies

Simmer chicken breasts until cooked; season if desired.
Reserve the water that the chicken simmered in for sauce.
Remove bones and cut chicken into small strips or cubes.
Allow 1 ounce chicken per enchilada.

Grate or cut your favorite cheese (or mixed cheeses) into
thin strips. Allow ½ ounce cheese per enchilada. Cut
Ortega whole green chilies into very thin strips and chop a
little for garnish on top (3½ ounces equal 37 calories).

Warm the sauce (see recipe on following page) in PAM-
sprayed or Teflon pan. Soften the tortillas in the sauce.
Remove tortillas from sauce and fill each with 1 ounce
chicken, ½ ounce cheese, and 1-2 strips of green chilies. If

desired, add 1 tablespoon of sauce and then roll. Make sure the tortilla is soft enough or it will crack when rolling. When pan is full, garnish with chopped chilies and grated cheese or 1-2 olives, but don't forget to count the calories. Bake at 350° for 20-30 minutes, until cheese is melted and toasty on top. Serves 8.

Sauce

Reserved liquid that chicken simmered in plus
    enough water to equal 21 ounces
1 can Campbell's cream of chicken soup, undiluted
Chili powder, to taste
Ground cumin, to taste
Oregano, to taste
Garlic powder, to taste
Onion powder, to taste
Seasoned salt, to taste
2 tablespoons cornstarch

Combine seasonings with broth. Thicken with the cornstarch. Yield: 64 tablespoons (4 cups) sauce at 5½ calories per tablespoon. Unused sauce may be frozen for later use.

Calories per serving/**370**
(2 enchiladas)

---

*"God does not get discouraged when
it takes a long time."*

Lemon Chicken Cutlets

1 7-ounce chicken breast, split, boned and skinned
1 slice bread, crumbled
2 tablespoons Parmesan cheese
½ tablespoon diet margarine, melted
Dash paprika
Dash pepper
Dash garlic powder

In a pie pan, combine bread crumbs, cheese, paprika, pepper, and garlic powder. Mix thoroughly. Lightly brush chicken with melted margarine and roll in the cheese-crumb mixture. Arrange in a PAM-sprayed baking pan. Bake uncovered in a 400° oven for 15 minutes or microwave on "high" for 5-7 minutes.

Sauce

1 tablespoon diet margarine
¼ pound fresh mushrooms, sliced
2 tablespoons lemon juice
½ tablespoon chopped fresh parsley
¼ teaspoon dry whole rosemary
½ teaspoon grated lemon peel

While the chicken is baking, melt the diet margarine in a small PAM-sprayed skillet. Add mushrooms and cook until mushrooms are golden (slightly firm, not limp). Stir in lemon juice, parsley, rosemary, and lemon peel. Heat to simmering. As soon as the chicken is done, remove from oven and place on a serving platter. Cover with sauce. Serve immediately. Serves 2.

Calories per serving/**295**

Tuna Casserole

1 6½-ounce can tuna, drained and flaked
2 ounces dry spaghetti, cooked until slightly firm
1 4-ounce can mushrooms, drained
1 stalk celery, chopped
½ tomato, finely diced
2 tablespoons minced onion
1 tablespoon Worcestershire sauce
¼ teaspoon garlic powder
⅔ cup nonfat milk
2 ounces Cheddar cheese, shredded
3 Saltine crackers, crumbled

Cook the spaghetti; drain. Add milk and stir. Combine with tuna, mushrooms, celery, tomato, onion, and seasonings. Put into a 1½-quart Pyrex casserole dish. Mix the cheese and cracker crumbs; sprinkle on top of the casserole. Cover and bake at 375° for 25 minutes. Serves 4.

Calories per serving/**188**

Tuna Sandwich

2 ounces tuna, water-packed
1 tablespoon OV mayonnaise*
1 tablespoon sweet pickle relish
1 tablespoon celery, chopped
Chopped onion, to taste
1 slice bread

Mix tuna, mayonnaise, pickle relish, celery, and onion. Spread bread with small amount of mayonnaise. Top with tuna mixture. Yield: 1 open-face sandwich. One serving.

Calories per serving/**206**

(Add 70 calories for additional slice of bread.)

*See page 52.

Tuna Cheese Bean Casserole

¾ cup tuna, water-packed
1 cup French-style green beans
½ cup juice from green beans
2 slices American cheese

Place all ingredients in a small saucepan and cook at medium heat until cheese is melted. *Makes a good lunch.* Serves 2.

Calories per serving/**166**

Summer Tuna Cakes

1 medium zucchini, finely shredded
1 6½-ounce can tuna, drained
3 slices (1½ cups) bread, crumbled
1 egg
2 teaspoons grated onion
1 teaspoon lemon juice
¼ teaspoon salt
¼ teaspoon pepper
2 slices whole-wheat bread
3 tablespoons OV mayonnaise*
2 large lettuce leaves
1 small tomato, sliced

Pat zucchini dry with paper towels. In medium bowl, mix zucchini with tuna, bread crumbs, egg, onion, lemon juice, salt, and pepper. Shape the zucchini mixture into two 3-inch round patties. In 10-inch PAM-sprayed skillet, cook patties over medium heat until browned on both sides, about 8-10 minutes.

Toast whole-wheat slices. On 2 individual plates, slice whole-wheat toast diagonally in ½. Spread with mayonnaise. Top with a lettuce leaf, ½ the tomato slices, and a

*See page 52.

tuna patty. To omit the extra bread, lay lettuce on each plate, place circle of tomato slices on lettuce, and place tuna patty on top. Add a dollop mayonnaise, if desired. *Summer Tuna Cakes make a delicious main meal.* Simply add vegetables. Serves 2.

Calories per serving/**382**

Tuna Chili

1-2 cups tomato juice
1 6-ounce can tuna, drained
1 teaspoon onion flakes
1-2 teaspoons chili powder
1 small can French-style green beans, drained
1 small can mushrooms, drained (optional)

Heat tomato juice, onion flakes, and chili powder. Add tuna, green beans, and mushrooms. Simmer 10 minutes. *Delicious!* Serves 2.

Calories per serving/**192**

"Definition of BECOME: to come or grow to be. When I enter God's personal service, I become, I come or grow to be what I ought to be— an example of HIS RIGHTEOUSNESS."

Orange Juice Poached Fish

2 cups orange juice
2 tablespoons pickling spices
½ teaspoon salt (optional)
4 slices (16 ounces) halibut, cod, snapper, or other fish
1 tablespoon cornstarch (optional)

In a large heavy skillet, combine orange juice, pickling spices, and salt. Heat to simmer (do not boil). Add fish. Cover and simmer 10 minutes until fish flakes easily when tested with a fork. Remove from heat. Keep warm. If desired, stir cornstarch into a little cold water and stir into orange juice until thickened; serve with fish. Serves 4.

Calories per serving/**181**

Egg Foo Yong

4 eggs
½ teaspoon salt
1 6-ounce can water chestnuts, halved
½ small onion, diced
1 16-ounce can bean sprouts, drained
1 4½-ounce can broken pieces of shrimp, drained
1 tablespoon margarine

Put eggs, salt, water chestnuts, onion, and bean sprouts into blender. Cover and blend at high speed until well-blended. Stir in shrimp.* Melt margarine in fry pan or on griddle. Using ¼-cup measure per patty, pour onto greased surface. Turn when browned. Place on warmed serving platter. Serve with cocktail sauce. Yield: 10 patties. Serves 5.

Calories per serving/**156**
(2 *patties*)

---

*Chicken or cubed beef may be substituted for shrimp.

Shrimp Creole

1 cup (or more) sliced fresh mushrooms
1 cup sliced celery
½ cup barbecue sauce
2 cups fresh tomatoes or 1 1-pound can tomatoes
½ cup finely chopped onions
1 teaspoon salt
1½ pounds cooked shrimp

Steam celery until bright. Add mushrooms to steamer.
Combine barbecue sauce, tomatoes, onions, and salt. Heat
until bubbly. Add celery, mushrooms, and shrimp. Serve
over ½ cup cooked brown rice per serving. Serves 6.

Calories per serving/**146**
*(Add 152 calories for ⅔ cup brown
rice.)*

Gioppino

1 clove garlic, crushed
½ onion, diced
2 drops Tabasco
1 cup diced tomatoes
1 cup water
Chopped parsley, to taste
1 bay leaf
Salt and pepper, to taste
3½ ounces shrimp
3½ ounces crabmeat

Saute garlic and onion in Teflon pan glazed with French
low-calorie dressing for 3-5 minutes. Add parsley, bay leaf,
salt, pepper, Tabasco, tomatoes, and water. Simmer 15
minutes. Add shrimp and crabmeat. Cook 15 minutes.
Serves 2.

Calories per serving/**185**

Poached Fish

8 ounces halibut, cod, or red snapper
1 tablespoon lemon juice
Salt and pepper, to taste
1 cup water

Combine water and lemon juice in skillet. Place rack in skillet. Season fish and place on rack. Cover. Cook until fish is tender, about 10 minutes. Serves 2.

Calories per serving/**67**

Shark Fillet (or any Fish Fillet)

2 tablespoons orange juice
2 tablespoons soy sauce
1 tablespoon oil
2 tablespoons catsup
1 green onion, chopped
8 ounces fish

Mix all ingredients except fish. Place fish and ½ sauce in shallow pan. Broil. Turn fish carefully and brush with remaining sauce. Broil until done. Serves 2.

Calories per serving/**225**

Mushroom Sandwich

1 4-ounce can chopped mushrooms
1 tablespoon dehydrated onions
1 tablespoon prepared mustard
¼ teaspoon thyme
1 ounce Parmesan cheese
1 ounce Monterey Jack cheese, sliced
1 slice bread, toasted

Mix mushrooms, onions, mustard, thyme, and Parmesan cheese. Place on toasted bread. Lightly spread with mustard. Top with Monterey Jack cheese. Place under broiler until cheese melts (or microwave on 80 for 1¼-1½ minutes). Serve with dill pickles, radishes, carrots. One serving.

Calories/**284**

"I was chosen, foreknown, sanctified, and consecrated to be OBEDIENT by the Holy Spirit to Jesus."

Skinny Scallop Kabob

1 pound scallops
½ teaspoon tarragon
½ cup lemon juice
1 tablespoon safflower oil
½ teaspoon salt or salt substitute
1 pound cucumber, cubed
2 tablespoons onion flakes
1 pound fresh mushrooms
½ pound asparagus spears, cut in thirds or halves

Preheat broiler or grill. Shuck, wash, and dry scallops. Mix
lemon juice, tarragon, oil, and salt (or salt substitute).
Marinate remaining ingredients in lemon juice mixture ½
hour. Thread 4 skewers with scallops and vegetables, alter-
nating ingredients until all are used. Broil 3 inches from
source of heat 5 minutes or until golden brown, or grill over
moderate heat 10 minutes, turning several times to brown
evenly. Baste with marinade during the cooking period.
Add salt (or salt substitute) and pepper to taste. Serves 4.

Calories per serving/**186**

Brown Rice Casserole

1 cup brown rice (may substitute small amount
  of wild rice)
2 tablespoons wheat kernels (optional)
2 tablespoons raw sunflower seeds (optional)
¼ cup chopped onion
1 cup chopped celery
Mushrooms, chopped (optional)
1 teaspoon seasoned salt
2 tablespoons butter
1 quart chicken broth

Combine all ingredients. Place in casserole. Bake, covered, at 325° for 2 hours. Check periodically to make sure that it does not bake dry. *Freezes well.* Serves 10.

Calories per serving/**110**

Italian Green Beans

½ cup tomato juice
Dash onion and garlic powder
½ teaspoon onion flakes
½ teaspoon oregano
1 teaspoon chopped green pepper
½-1 cup green beans
2 ounces Mozzarella cheese
1 slice bread, toasted and crumbled

Mix tomato juice, onion, garlic powder, onion flakes, oregano, and green pepper. Cook until thick sauce. Place green beans in PAM-sprayed small baking dish. Pour ¾ of the toasted bread crumbs over beans. Add the Mozzarella cheese. Top with remaining toasted bread crumbs. Pour sauce over top. Bake 15 minutes at 375°. One serving.

Calories/**312**

Copenhagen Cabbage Casserole

1 pound lean ground beef
¼ onion, minced
1 16-ounce can tomato juice
⅛ teaspoon cinnamon
⅛ teaspoon ground cloves
1 teaspoon salt
Sweetener, to taste
1 medium head (4 cups) cabbage, shredded

Brown meat and onion together; drain off fat. In large bowl, mix tomato juice, cinnamon, ground cloves, salt, and sweetener. Stir in meat and onion mixture. Add cabbage. Mix well. Place in casserole. Cover and bake at 350° for 45 minutes. Serves 4.

Calories per serving/**250**

Zucchini Lasagna

1 pound hamburger
1 medium onion, finely chopped
1 28-ounce can tomatoes (plus liquid), chopped
1 6-ounce can tomato paste
1 4-ounce can mushrooms, drained
1 teaspoon garlic powder
2 teaspoons Italian seasoning
2 large zucchinis, sliced lengthwise about ¼ inch thick
6 ounces Mozzarella cheese, shredded
8 ounces Ricotta cheese
2 ounces Parmesan cheese, grated

Brown hamburger with onion; drain. Add tomatoes and liquid, tomato paste, mushrooms, garlic powder, and Italian seasoning. Cover and simmer 1 hour. Steam or microwave zucchini slices until barely fork-tender. In a 9×13-inch

PAM-sprayed pan, place the following ingredients in layers: ½ meat sauce, zucchini slices, ½ cheeses, ½ meat sauce, and ½ cheeses. Cover with foil and bake at 350° for 1½ hours. Remove cover for the last 10 minutes of baking period. Serves 12.

Calories per serving/**220**

Eggplant Appetizer

2 cups onion bouillon
½ teaspoon Italian seasoning
4 cups unpeeled diced eggplant
2 cups sliced celery
1 cup tomato puree
¼ cup vinegar
4 teaspoons capers

In saucepan, combine onion bouillon and Italian seasoning. Bring to a boil. Add eggplant and celery. Reduce heat, simmer 10 minutes until vegetables are tender; drain. Combine tomato puree, vinegar, and capers; pour over eggplant and celery. Toss lightly until well-mixed. Refrigerate 1 hour, until chilled. Serves 4.

Calories per serving/**78**

Spinach Gnocchi

1 10-ounce package frozen spinach, thawed,
   squeezed dry, and chopped
12 ounces Ricotta cheese
2 eggs
3 tablespoons Parmesan cheese
3 green onions, finely minced
¼ teaspoon garlic powder
½ teaspoon pepper
¼ teaspoon nutmeg
4 slices bread, crumbled

In a deep bowl, combine all ingredients and stir; it will be a somewhat stiff mixture. Roll teaspoons of mixture in your hand to measure 1½ inches in length. Place gnocchi on a plate. Pour water into a large saucepan until ⅔ full; boil. Add 12 gnocchi and cook for 5 minutes. Remove the gnocchi with a slotted spoon and place on a plate. Repeat with remaining gnocchi. The gnocchi may be covered and refrigerated at this point.

Sauce

1 can tomato sauce
¼ cup water
1 teaspoon Italian seasoning

In small pan, combine ingredients and simmer 20 minutes.

To serve, pour sauce into a 9×13-inch cake pan. Arrange gnocchi in a single layer on top of sauce. Sprinkle with 2 tablespoons Parmesan cheese and 2 tablespoons chopped parsley. Bake in 350° oven for 10 minutes.
Yield: 70-75 gnocchi. Serves 6.

Calories per serving/**205**
*(approximately 12 gnocchi,
including sauce and topping)*

Cold Stuffed Zucchini Boats

1 extra-large zucchini
1 stalk celery, finely chopped
2 ounces chicken or turkey, cooked and cubed
1 green onion, finely chopped
⅔ cup cottage cheese, creamed in a blender
½ teaspoon lime juice
1 teaspoon curry powder
¼ teaspoon ground ginger

Divide zucchini in ½. Steam until tender or wrap in Saran Wrap and microwave on "high" 4 minutes. Scoop out the insides and discard. Chill shell thoroughly. In a medium bowl, combine celery, green onion, and meat. In another bowl, combine cottage cheese, lime juice, curry powder, and ground ginger. Stir. Pour over meat mixture. Blend well. Chill. When ready to serve, ladle into the 2 cooled hollowed zucchini boats. Serves 2.

Calories per serving/**151**

Skillet Zucchini

2 zucchinis, sliced into ¼- to ½-inch rounds
2 tomatoes, sliced
¼ cup chopped onions
1 ounce Cheddar cheese, grated
1 ounce Mozzarella cheese, grated

Place zucchini in bottom of skillet. Top with sliced tomatoes and chopped onion. Cover and cook over low heat until zucchini is medium-tender. Top vegetables with grated cheeses. Leave lid off and turn heat up to medium-high. Cook until moisture evaporates and cheese melts. One serving.

Calories/**225**

Vegetable Kabobs

1 small (¾ pound) eggplant, unpeeled
  and cut into 2-inch cubes
2 large carrots, cut into ½-inch slices
12 small thin-skinned potatoes
3 medium zucchinis, cut crosswise into 1-inch slices
2 small red or green bell peppers, seeded and cut
  into 1-inch squares
1 large onion, cut into wedges and layers separated
16 large whole mushrooms
Herb marinade (See following page.)
Salt, to taste

Cook eggplant in 1 inch of boiling water for 3 minutes;
drain. Cook carrots in boiling water until tender-crisp,
about 6 minutes; drain. Cook unpeeled potatoes in boiling
water until tender, about 20 minutes; drain and cut in ½.

Place eggplant, carrots, potatoes, zucchinis, bell peppers,
onion, and mushrooms in a plastic bag. Prepare herb
marinade (following page) and pour it over the vegetables. Seal the bag and refrigerate 2 hours or overnight.

Drain and reserve marinade from vegetables. Onto 8 sturdy
metal skewers, alternately thread vegetables. Place on a
lightly greased grill 4-6 inches above a solid bed of low-
glowing coals. Cook, turning often and basting with
reserved marinade, for 15-20 minutes, until vegetables are
tender. Sprinkle lightly with salt before serving. Serves 4.

Herb Marinade

¾ cup salad oil
¼ cup white vinegar
2 cloves garlic, minced or pressed
1 teaspoon Dijon mustard
1 teaspoon dry basil
1 teaspoon oregano leaves
½ teaspoon marjoram leaves
½ teaspoon dry rosemary
¼ teaspoon pepper

Combine all ingredients.

Calories per serving/**385**
(*vegetables plus marinade*)

Eggplant Mozzarella

9 ounces eggplant, peeled and cut into 3 thick slices
1 teaspoon margarine
3 ounces (3 slices) Mozzarella cheese
1 8-ounce can tomato sauce
¼ cup water
1 teaspoon Italian seasoning
⅛ teaspoon garlic powder

Baste 1 side of each eggplant slice with margarine. Broil about 5 minutes, until browned. Turn the eggplant slices over; baste and broil. While eggplant is broiling, heat the tomato sauce, water, and seasonings; simmer 20 minutes. When eggplant is browned, top with cheese and place under broiler until cheese is melted. Transfer to a serving plate and cover with sauce. Serves 3.

Calories per serving/**160**

Chilies Rellenos

1 7-ounce can whole green chilies
1 egg, separated
1½ tablespoons water
2 ounces Monterey Jack cheese
1 slice bread, crumbled
1 cup V-8 juice

Remove seeds and wash chilies. Cut cheese into strips and stuff into chilies. Beat egg white until very stiff. Mix egg yolk with water and gently fold into egg white. Add bread crumbs and stir. Place batter in a small casserole dish and add whole chilies, covering them with the batter. Chill ½ hour. Heat V-8 juice in a large PAM-sprayed skilled. Add chilies and batter. Simmer with the lid on 10 minutes; cheese will melt. Serves 2.

Calories per serving/**174**

Eggplant Frittata

9 eggs
1 tablespoon water
8 ounces (2 cups) eggplant, peeled and cubed (pea-size)
2 slices bread, crumbled
1 tablespoon margarine
½ cup V-8 juice
2 ounces (½ cup) Mozzarella cheese, shredded
¼ cup Parmesan cheese
¼ teaspoon garlic powder
Dash black pepper

In a medium bowl, combine and beat 1 egg and water. Add eggplant and toss. Let stand 10 minutes and then drain. Sprinkle in the crumbs and toss.

In a 10-inch PAM-sprayed skillet, melt margarine and cook

eggplant 5 minutes, until browned. Combine the 8 remaining eggs, V-8 juice, Mozzarella cheese, Parmesan cheese, garlic powder, and pepper. Beat until thoroughly blended. Pour over eggplant and cook 12-15 minutes over medium heat, until eggs are set. Cover, remove from heat, and let stand 10 minutes. If eggs are not set, place under broiler for a few minutes. Serves 4-6.

Calories per serving:
Recipe divided into 4/**321**
Recipe divided into 6/**214**

Spinach Soufflé

1 10-ounce package frozen chopped spinach
1 slice bread, crumbled
1¼ cups skim milk
½ teaspoon salt
⅛ teaspoon pepper
⅛ teaspoon nutmeg
1 small onion, finely chopped
1 teaspoon Worcestershire sauce
4 egg yolks
5 egg whites
1 tablespoon lemon juice

Defrost spinach; drain thoroughly. In saucepan, combine spinach, bread, milk, salt, pepper, nutmeg, onion, and Worcestershire sauce. Stir well. Heat until boiling. Beat in egg yolks one at a time; cook until slightly thickened. Remove from heat. Beat egg whites with lemon juice until stiff, but not dry; fold ¼ into spinach mixture thoroughly, then fold in remainder. Heap mixture into collared 6-cup soufflé dish. Bake in 375° oven until puffed and golden brown, about 35 minutes. Serve immediately. Serve with crisp green salad or fresh tomato slices, celery, and carrot sticks. Serves 4.

Calories per serving/**144**

Potato Casserole

8 small (1½ pounds) red potatoes, boiled or steamed
⅔ cup low-fat cottage cheese
1 tablespoon dried parsley flakes
¼ cup liquid skim milk
½ cup chopped green onions or chives
Salt and pepper, to taste

Slice potatoes into bowl. Combine with cottage cheese, parsley, skim milk, green onions (or chives), salt, and pepper. Put into greased casserole and bake at 350° for 25-30 minutes. Serves 2.

Calories per serving/**165**

Halibut Italiano

1 4-ounce halibut fillet
½ cup fresh whole mushrooms (for garnish)
½ cup spaghetti sauce
½ ounce Parmesan cheese

Place fish fillet in baking dish. Garnish with mushrooms. Pour spaghetti sauce over all. Sprinkle with Parmesan cheese. Bake at 350° for ½ hour, until firm. One serving.

Calories/**278**

Skinny Lady Scramble

1 package (10 ounces) frozen spinach
3 tablespoons onion flakes
1½ pounds ground round steak
Salt and pepper, to taste
5 eggs, well-beaten

Cook spinach; drain (press in sieve to remove all water). Saute ground round steak until it loses its color. Stir in onion, spinach, salt, and pepper. Add eggs. Scramble, cooking until eggs are set, and serve. Serves 6-8.

Calories per serving:
Recipe divided into 8/**215**
Recipe divided into 6/**287**

Crustless Seafood Quiche

2 4-6 ounce cans any combination of tuna, shrimp,
    crab, or lobster, rinsed and drained
1 small onion, finely diced
1 teaspoon butter or margarine
1 cup shredded Cheddar, Colby, Swiss, or
    any other hard cheese
2 cups milk or half-and-half
2 eggs, lightly beaten
2 slices (1 cup) bread, crumbled (Remove crusts.)
½ teaspoon salt
⅛ teaspoon white pepper

Rinse seafood and drain well on paper towel. Briefly sauté onion in butter, until soft. Flake seafood into 9-inch greased pie plate. Top with cheese and sautéed onion. Add milk to beaten eggs and stir in bread crumbs. Let stand 10 minutes. Pour egg, milk, and bread-crumb mixture over food in pie plate. Sprinkle with paprika. Bake at 350° about 45 minutes, until set and lightly browned. Cool 5 minutes, then cut into 6 wedges. Serves 6.

Calories per serving/**308**

Tostada Quiche

1 flour tortilla (8 inches in diameter)
1½ ounces Monterey Jack cheese, shredded
1 green onion, chopped
2 eggs
½ cup nonfat milk
⅛ teaspoon dry mustard
⅛ teaspoon chili powder
Dash liquid hot sauce or taco sauce

Warm and soften the tortilla by heating on griddle or heavy pan and flipping it several times, or place tortilla in a plastic bag and microwave it on "high" 10 seconds. Carefully fit the tortilla into the bottom of a round PAM-sprayed 1½- to 2-cup ramekin or oven-proof bowl. Sprinkle cheese into tortilla and top with green onion. In a small bowl, beat the other ingredients and carefully pour them into the tortilla. Bake at 375° for 25-30 minutes. Cool for a few minutes. Divide in ½ and serve. Serves 2.

Calories per serving/**250**

Zucchini Quiche

1 pound zucchini, sliced
6 ounces Mozzarella cheese, shredded
1 cup Ricotta cheese
½ cup nonfat milk
3 eggs
¼ teaspoon ground oregano
¼ teaspoon basil leaves, crushed
¼ teaspoon garlic powder
⅛ teaspoon black pepper

PAM-spray a 10-inch skillet. Saute zucchini slices until
barely tender. Arrange ¾ of the slices in a 9-inch pie pan.
Sprinkle Mozzarella cheese over the zucchini. In a bowl,
mix the Ricotta cheese and eggs until smooth. Add milk,
oregano, basil, garlic, and black pepper. Pour ingredients
in bowl over the zucchini and cheese. Arrange remaining
zucchini slices on top. Bake at 350° for 45 minutes, until
knife inserted in the center comes out clean. Cool for a few
minutes. Serves 6.

Calories per serving/**216**

Egg Salad Unsandwich

2 hard-cooked eggs, chopped
¼ cup cottage cheese
A few alfalfa sprouts
Enough mustard and yogannaise (2 parts yogurt
    and 1 part mayonnaise) to make it stick together
Lemon pepper seasoning, to taste
Lettuce leaves

Roll eggs, cottage cheese, alfalfa sprouts, mustard,
yogannaise, and lemon pepper seasoning into lettuce
leaves or serve on top of lettuce. One serving.

Calories/**150**

Crepe Fold-Overs

2 eggs
¼ teaspoon salt

In a small mixing bowl, beat eggs and salt well. Generously
spray large unheated Teflon saucepan with PAM. Pour
mixture into the unheated pan, covering the bottom evenly.
Place over medium heat. When the mixture bubbles and is
completely set, carefully turn it over. Turn crepe again
occasionally, until browned and partially crisp on edges.
Fill with your favorite "skinny" recipe ingredients (e.g.,
diced green pepper, onion, and tomato; or use following
broccoli and cheese recipe). Fold over. Add more filling on
top. Serves 4.

Calories per serving/**41**

Broccoli and Cheese Crepe Filling

12 ounces (1½ cup) Ricotta cheese
3 small stems and flowerets (2 cups) broccoli,
    cooked and coarsely chopped
½ cup finely chopped green onions
¼ teaspoon garlic powder
¼ teaspoon sweetener
¼ teaspoon salt
2 ounces (¼ cup) Parmesan cheese, grated

Combine all ingredients except Parmesan cheese. Mix
well in a large bowl. Spoon evenly into center of each crepe
(see Crepe Fold-Overs recipe). Fold both sides of crepe
toward center and place seam side down in glass baking
dish. Sprinkle the Parmesan cheese evenly. Bake at 350° for
20 minutes, until Parmesan cheese is lightly browned.
Serves 4.

Calories per serving/**251**
*(crepe plus filling; filling alone
is 210 calories)*

Brunch Cheese Casserole

3 slices bread, crusts removed
6 ounces Cheddar cheese, grated
4 eggs
1 teaspoon salt
1 teaspoon dry mustard
2 cups skim milk

Spray 9-inch square casserole with PAM. Cut bread into squares and spread in bottom of pan. Cover with Cheddar cheese. Beat eggs, salt, and mustard; add to milk and mix. Pour over cheese and bread. Sprinkle with paprika. Refrigerate 12 hours before baking. Bake uncovered 1 hour at 325°. Garnish with crumbled bacon if desired (add calories). Allow to set 10-15 minutes before cutting and serving. Serves 6.

Calories per serving/**230**

"Standing before the Lord and choosing
His way brings—
RELIEF, REPENTANCE,
REST, and RESTORATION."

Taking Care of Cheese

COOKING

All cheese dishes should be cooked at a low temperature and in a short amount of time. Excessive heat and overcooking cause fat separation, stringing, and toughening of the cheese.

STORAGE

Hard cheese such as Cheddar, Swiss, and Parmesan may be kept for several weeks. Soft cheese such as cream, cottage, and Neufchatel is highly perishable and should be used within a few days after purchase.

Cheese should be refrigerated at 35-40°. It can be wrapped in the original wrapper for refrigeration. Cut surfaces should be covered tightly with wax paper, foil, or plastic to protect the surface from drying out. Tightly covered refrigerator dishes are excellent for storage, especially for strong-smelling cheese.

For its most distinct flavor, most cheese should be served at room temperature. Cream, cottage, and Neufchatel cheese should be chilled when served.

FREEZING CHEESE

If pieces of cheese are larger than ½ pound, they should be cut into smaller pieces and wrapped tightly. Use a moisture-proof wrapper to prevent evaporation. For small pieces of cheese, the original package may be used if the package is airtight. Freeze quickly at 0° or lower. Slow thawing in a refrigerator in the unopened package is recommended. Use cheese as soon as possible after thawing is complete.

Some varieties that may be frozen are Brick, Camembert, Cheddar, Edam, Liederkranz, Mozzarella, Muenster, Parmesan, Port du Salut, Provolone, Romano, and Swiss. Some Limburger, Colby, Gouda, and Club cheese will freeze well, while others will become crumbly and mealy. Blue, Gorgonzola, and Roquefort may become crumbly, but will be suitable for salads. Freezing will affect the texture of such soft cheese as cream, creamed cottage, and processed cheese.

Recommended Cheese and Fruit Combinations

Cheddar cheese and Jonathan apples; Swiss cheese and Greening apples or Green Finger grapes; Blue cheese and Anjou or Bosc pears; Brick cheese and Tokay grapes; Gouda cheese and Golden Delicious apples; Provolone cheese and Bartlett pears.

Cheese Chart

Cheese	Origin	Consistency and Texture	Color and Shape
Blue	France	Semisoft; visible veins of mold, pasty, sometimes crumbly	White, marbled with blue-green mold; cylindrical
Brick	United States	Semisoft; smooth, waxy body	Light yellow to orange; brick-shaped
Brie	France	Soft; thin edible crust, creamy interior	Whitish crust, creamy yellow interior; medium and small wheels
Camembert	France	Soft; thin edible crust, creamy interior	White crust, creamy yellow interior; small wheels
Cheddar (American)	England	Hard; smooth, firm body	Light yellow to orange; varied shapes and styles, with rind and rindless
Colby	United States	Hard type but softer and more open in texture than Cheddar	Light yellow to orange; cylindrical
Cottage	Uncertain	Soft, moist, delicate, large or small curds	White; packaged in cuplike containers
Cream	United States	Soft; smooth, buttery	White; foil-wrapped in rectangular portions
Edam	Holland	Hard type but softer than Cheddar; more open, mealy body	Creamy yellow with red wax coat; cannonball shape
Gouda	Holland	Hard type but softer than Cheddar; more open, mealy body like Edam	Creamy yellow with or without red wax coat; round and flat
Gruyere	Switzerland	Hard; tiny gas holes or eyes	Light yellow; flat wheels
Limburger	Belgium	Soft; smooth, waxy body	Creamy white; rectangular
Monterey (Jack)	United States	Semisoft; smooth, open open texture	Creamy white wheels
Mozzarella (Pizza Cheese)	Italy	Semisoft; plastic	Creamy white; rectangular and spherical
Muenster	Germany	Semisoft; smooth, waxy body	Yellow tan or white surface, creamy white interior; small wheels and blocks
Neufchatel	France	Soft; smooth, creamy	White; foil-wrapped in rectangular retail portions
Parmesan (Reggiano)	Italy	Hard grating; granular, brittle body	Light yellow with brown or black coatings; cylindrical
Port du Salut (Oka)	Trappist Monks, France, Canada	Semisoft; smooth, buttery	Russet surface, creamy yellow interior; small wheels
Primost	Norway	Semisoft	Light brown; cubical and cylindrical
Provolone	Italy	Hard; compact, flaky	Yellow to golden-brown surface, bound with cord, yellowish-white interior; pear and sausage shapes
Ricotta	Italy	Soft; moist and grainy, or dry	White; packaged fresh in paper, plastic, or metal containers, or dry for grating
Roquefort (Blue Cheese)	France	Semisoft; visible veins of mold, pasty and sometimes crumbly	White, marbled with blue-green molds; cylindrical
Swiss	Switzerland	Hard; smooth, with large gas holes or eyes	Rindless blocks and large wheels with rind

Flavor	Basic Ingredient	Mode of Serving	Caloric Value per Ounce
Piquant, spicy	Cows' milk, whole	As such (dessert); in dips; in cooked foods; in salads	100
Mild	Cows' milk, whole	As such; in sandwiches, salads	105
Mild to pungent	Cows' milk, whole	As such (dessert)	94
Mild to pungent	Cows' milk, whole	As such (dessert)	30
Mild to sharp	Cows' milk, whole	As such; in sandwiches; in cooked foods	85
Mild	Cows' milk, whole	As such; in sandwiches; in cooked foods	105
Mild, slightly acid	Cows' milk, skimmed; cream dressing may be added	As such; in salads; in dips; in cooked foods	110
Mild, slightly acid	Cream and cows' milk, whole	As such; in sandwiches; in salads; on crackers	100
Mild, nutlike	Cows' milk, partly skimmed	As such; on crackers; with fresh fruit	100
Mild, nutlike, similar	Cows' milk, partly skimmed but more milk fat than Edam	As such; on crackers; with fresh fruit	105
Nutlike, sweetish	Cows' milk, usually partly skimmed	As such (dessert)	107
Robust, highly aromatic	Cows' milk, whole or partly skimmed	In sandwiches; on crackers	98
Mild	Cows' milk, whole	As such; in sandwiches	102
Mild, delicate	Cows' milk, whole or partly skimmed	As such; in pizza and other cooked foods	95
Mild to mellow, between Brick and Limburger	Cows' milk, whole	As such; in sandwiches	95
Mild	Cows' milk, whole	As such; in sandwiches; in dips; in salads	69
Sharp, piquant	Cows' milk, partly skimmed	As such; as seasoning (grated)	110
Mellow to robust, between Cheddar and Limburger	Cows' milk, whole and slightly acid	As such (dessert); with fresh fruit	100
Mild, sweetish, caramel	Whey with added buttermilk, whole milk or cream	As such; in cooked foods	134
Mild to sharp and piquant, usually smoked	Cows' milk, whole	As such; in cooked foods	95
Bland but semisweet	Whey and whole or skimmed milk, or partly skimmed milk	As such; in cooked foods; as seasoning when dried	47
Sharp, spicy, piquant	Sheeps' milk	As such (dessert); in salads; on crackers	105
Sweetish, nutlike	Cows' milk, partly skimmed	As such; in sandwiches; with salads	100

A Calorie Burned
Is a Calorie Burned!

A recent report by the Southern California Medical Association pointed out that proper weight control and physical fitness cannot be attained by dieting alone.

Many people who are engaged in sedentary occupations do not realize that calories can be burned by the hundreds by engaging in strenuous exercises that do not require physical exercise. The following is a list of calorie-burning activities and the number of calories per hour they consume:

Beating around the bush ...75
Jumping to conclusions ...100
Climbing the walls 150
Passing the buck 25
Throwing your weight
   around 300
Dragging your heels 100
Pushing your luck 250
Making mountains out of
   molehills 500
Wading through
   paperwork 300
Bending over backwards ...75
Balancing the books 23
Running around
   in circles 350
Eating crow 225
Tooting your own horn 25
Hitting the nail on
   the head 50
—Anonymous contributor

VEGETABLES

The Artichoke

How to Choose Artichokes

Select artichokes that feel heavy and which look plump and fresh. Avoid any with loose or spreading leaves.

Artichokes are bright green in the spring months. They may appear bronzed in winter. These are "winter-kissed" by frost, which improves the flavor, if anything.

Sauces for Artichokes

Creamy
Italian Dip

No-Calorie
French Dressing

Buttermilk
Dressing

OV Mayonnaise

Calories/**30**
(average size)

Anatomy of an Artichoke

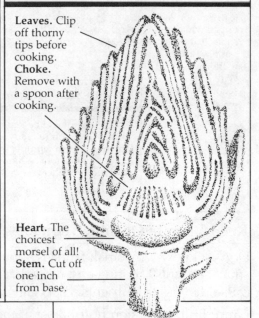

Leaves. Clip off thorny tips before cooking.
Choke. Remove with a spoon after cooking.

Heart. The choicest morsel of all!
Stem. Cut off one inch from base.

Basic Preparation

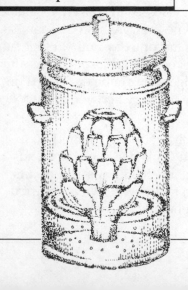

Wash and trim as described above. Stand artichoke upright in deep saucepan. Add ¼ teaspoon salt for each artichoke. Add 2-3 inches boiling water. Cover and boil gently 35-45 minutes. Lift out and drain upside down. (Stainless steel, enamel, or copper cookware will not darken cut surfaces.)

How to Eat an Artichoke

Pull off leaves 1 at a time and dip each into a sauce. Pull each leaf through closed teeth. Discard tough end of leaf. Eat purple-tipped white cone all at once, same way as with leaves. With a spoon, scoop out and discard the fuzzy choke.

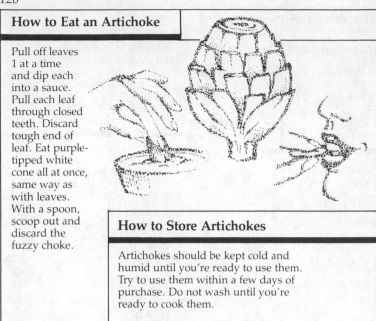

How to Store Artichokes

Artichokes should be kept cold and humid until you're ready to use them. Try to use them within a few days of purchase. Do not wash until you're ready to cook them.

Keep Vitamins in Your Vegetables

Do you know why small families should cook vegetables in small amounts? Storing and reheating cooked vegetables cause the loss of nutrients, especially vitamin C.

Grace Brill, extension nutritionist at the University of Minnesota, says that vitamin C losses in cooked vegetables increase with the length of time they are stored. They have about ¾ as much vitamin C after one day in the refrigerator as when freshly cooked. Cooked vegetables reheated after two or three days in the refrigerator can be depended on for only ⅓-½ as much vitamin C as when you first cooked them.

Foods from the vegetable-fruit group are counted on to provide nearly all the vitamin C needed each day. Thus vegetables such as asparagus, broccoli, Brussels sprouts, cabbage, and spinach, which make worthwhile contributions of vitamin C, should generally be cooked in the amounts eaten at one meal.

Asparagus Tips Vinaigrette

2 cups asparagus tips
1 quart boiling salted water

Cook asparagus in boiling salted water until barely tender. Drain and chill.

Vinaigrette Dressing

1 teaspoon onion flakes
¼ teaspoon mustard
⅛ teaspoon salt
1 tablespoon safflower oil
2 tablespoons white vinegar

Combine all ingredients. Chill. Pour over asparagus tips before serving. Serves 4.

Calories per serving/**50**

Spinach Broccoli Combo

1 package (10 ounces) frozen chopped spinach
1 package (10 ounces) frozen chopped broccoli
⅔ cup water
1 teaspoon salt
1 tablespoon lemon juice

In covered saucepan, heat spinach, broccoli, water, and salt to boiling, breaking vegetables apart. Reduce heat; cook 5-10 minutes, until vegetables are tender. Drain. Toss with lemon juice. Serves 6.

Calories per serving/**30**

Marinated Mushrooms

1 8-ounce can button mushrooms
2 cloves garlic, peeled and halved
2 tablespoons olive oil
4 teaspoons red wine vinegar
1 teaspoon Worcestershire sauce
1 drop Tabasco sauce
⅛ teaspoon salt

Drain mushrooms, reserving liquid. Place ½ of the mushrooms in a glass jar and put ½ clove garlic on top of them. Add remaining mushrooms and put another ½ clove garlic on top. Mix all other ingredients together and pour over mushrooms. Add enough liquid from the mushrooms to cover them. Shake jar to mix well and store in the refrigerator. Allow mushrooms to marinate 24 hours before serving. Put a toothpick in each mushroom and serve on plate. Serves 4.

Calories per serving/**110**

Tangy Mustard Beans

2 10-ounce packages green beans
¾ teaspoon seasoned salt
2 teaspoons Grey Poupon brown mustard
2 tablespoons safflower oil
3 tablespoons vinegar
½ teaspoon Sugar Twin (or another sugar substitute to
   equal ½ teaspoon sugar)

Put beans, water, and salt substitute into medium saucepan; cover and bring to a boil over moderately high heat. Reduce heat to medium and cook 5 minutes. In small bowl, mix remaining ¼ teaspoon salt substitute, mustard, oil, vinegar, and sugar substitute; add to undrained beans and stir to coat beans completely. Leftover beans may be refrigerated. *They are delicious cold!* Serves 4.

Calories per serving/**53½**
(1 cup)

Quick Broiled Tomatoes

1 medium tomato
1 teaspoon sweetener
Cinnamon, to taste

Cut tomato in ½. Sprinkle with cinnamon and ½ teaspoon sweetener. Broil about 10 minutes, approximately 5 inches from the heat source. One serving.

Calories/**35**

Vegetable Delight

Fresh vegetables, your choice
½ cup water
Mushrooms, sliced
Onion flakes, to taste
Schilling Salad Supreme, to taste
Seasoned salt substitute, to taste
Pepper, to taste
2 eggs
Leftover chicken, beef, or shrimp

In fry pan, steam vegetables in ¼ cup water until ½ done. If spinach is used, add just before other vegetables are ½ cooked. Add the mushrooms, onion flakes, Schilling Salad Supreme, seasoned salt substitute, and pepper. Beat the eggs and pour over the vegetables. Cover and simmer until done. Add leftover meat choice. One serving.

Calories/**Vary**
(depending upon ingredients used)

Zucchini Creole

1 pound zucchini, sliced
1 large tomato, skinned and chopped
¼ cup onion, chopped
1 tablespoon parsley, chopped
Seasoning, to taste

Combine all ingredients. Simmer over very low heat, without liquid, until zucchini is barely done. Serves 4.

Calories per serving/**34**

30-Calories-a-Cup Soup

6 bouillon cubes, any flavor
6 cups water
3 carrots, finely chopped
1 medium cabbage, finely chopped
2 stalks celery, finely chopped
1 onion, finely chopped, or ½ package onion soup mix
3½ cups fresh tomatoes, chopped, or No. 2½ can tomatoes

In saucepan, dissolve bouillon in 1 cup boiling water. Combine other ingredients (including remaining 5 cups water) with bouillon. Simmer 45 minutes, until soup thickens. A packet of beef stew seasoning or homemade or canned broth may be used in place of bouillon, but flavor and calorie count will differ. Serves 6.

Calories per serving/**30**
(1 cup)

Corn Medley

1 10-ounce package frozen corn
½ cup chopped celery
1 chicken bouillon cube
1 cup water
1 2-ounce can mushrooms
1 medium tomato, cut into thin wedges
Salt and pepper, to taste

Combine corn, celery, bouillon cube, and water; simmer until cube is dissolved and vegetables are tender. Add mushrooms, tomato, salt, and pepper. Simmer briefly. Serves 6.

Calories per serving/**50**

Mixed Vegetables Italian

2 tablespoons margarine
1 eggplant, cubed
1 cup zucchini, cubed
2 green peppers, cut into strips
1 cup fresh mushrooms, sliced
⅓ cup crushed tomatoes
2 10-ounce packages frozen pea pods
1 tablespoon soy sauce
Garlic powder, to taste
Basil leaves, to taste

Heat soy sauce and margarine in skillet or wok over medium high heat till margarine is melted. Then add vegetables and seasonings, adding water by tablespoons to keep vegetables from burning till heated through. Serves 8.

Calories per serving/**90**

Baked Potato

1 3-ounce mature baking potato,
   such as Idaho or russet

Preheat oven to 450°. Bake potato on oven rack 50 minutes.
When potato is ½ done, pierce with knife point to let
steam escape. Return to oven and finish baking. Test for
doneness by squeezing it to see if the potato is soft.

Gravy

¼ cup mushroom pieces, heated
1 teaspoon soy sauce

Mix mushrooms and soy sauce; pour over potato.
One serving.

Calories/**113**

Cheese-Stuffed Mushrooms

1 pound fresh mushrooms
1 small onion, minced
2 teaspoons butter or margarine
1 tablespoon minced parsley
4 tablespoons low-fat cottage cheese
3 tablespoons seasoned bread crumbs
Salt, to taste
Pepper, to taste
Garlic powder, to taste

Preheat broiler. Wash mushrooms and remove stems; chop
the stems and simmer 2 minutes in onions and butter. Add
parsley, cheese, and bread crumbs. Mix and season. Stuff
into mushroom caps and arrange on broiler pan. Broil until
lightly browned.

Calories per serving/**45**
(2 mushrooms)

Baked Zucchini

3 cups diced zucchini, boiled 5 minutes and drained
½ cup diced celery
½ cup chopped onion
1 teaspoon sage
1 teaspoon sweetener
½-1 teaspoon salt
½ cup low-fat or nonfat milk
1 large egg

Mix all ingredients and put into PAM-sprayed casserole.
Bake at 350° for 45-60 minutes. *Tastes like bread dressing.*
Serves 4.

Calories per serving/**49**

*"Once it was necessary to keep the law just
to reach Him. Now He reaches to us and enables us
to keep His commandments—and to
live in obedience."*

DESSERTS & BEVERAGES

All-Purpose Fruit-Filled Entree

Add to Diligence, in equal portions, 1 ingredient at a time:

Virtue
Knowledge
Temperance
Patience
Godliness
Brotherly affection
Christian love

Complete menu with Fruit Salad from Galatians 5:22-23.
Recipe found in 2 Peter 1:5-8.

Fruit Salad

1 portion Love
1 portion Joy
1 portion Peace
1 portion Long-Suffering
1 portion Kindness
1 portion Goodness
1 portion Faithfulness
1 portion Gentleness
1 portion Self-Control

Do not toss. Let all ingredients grow together.
From Galatians 5:22-23.

In this section we have included our beverage and punch recipes. We have not included any caloric values for sweetening, and you must remember to add them according to your choice of sweetener.

Try using fructose (12 calories per teaspoon) on fresh fruits as well as cooked-fruit recipes. It has surprising ability to enhance the flavor of the fruit.

Cranberry Juice Punch

1 quart cranberry juice
46 ounces pineapple juice
Sweetener, to taste
2 quarts sugar-free ginger ale

Combine chilled juices and sweetener. Add ice cubes.

Calories per serving/**76**
(1 cup)

Red Satin Punch

2 pints cranberry juice
1 quart apple juice
10 7-ounce bottles sugar-free 7-Up
2 trays sugar-free 7-Up ice cubes

Combine chilled juices. Slowly pour in 7-Up. Add 7-Up ice cubes. Serves 35.

Calories per serving/**31**

Citrus Cider

¼ cup pure grapefruit juice
¼ cup pure apple juice

Combine chilled juices. One serving.

Calories/**53**

Tart and Tangy Punch

1 pint pure grapefruit juice
1 pint grape juice
1 quart sugar-free 7-Up or ginger ale

Combine chilled juices and 7-Up (or ginger ale).
Add ice cubes.

Calories per serving/**22**
(½ cup)

Orange Jubilee

½ 6-ounce can frozen orange juice concentrate
½ cup nonfat dry milk powder
1 cup water
½ teaspoon vanilla
Sweetener, to taste
5-6 ice cubes, crushed

Combine all ingredients and blend in blender 30 seconds,
until smooth. Serve immediately. Serves 3.

Calories per serving/**133**
(1 cup)

Bedtime Snack Drink Mix

5 cups nonfat dry milk
5 teaspoons sweetener
⅛ envelope Butter Buds
⅛ teaspoon salt
½ teaspoon pumpkin pie spice

Mix all ingredients and store. For 1 serving, combine ⅓ cup Bedtime Snack Drink Mix with 1 cup boiling water. Stir. *Enjoy.*

Calories per serving/**81**
(1 cup)

Hot Spiced Tea

1 rounded teaspoon instant Nestea with tangy lemon flavor
Sweetener, to taste
⅛ teaspoon (or less) nutmeg
½ teaspoon pumpkin pie spice
¾-1 cup boiling water
2 ounces reconstituted frozen orange juice

In mug, combine Nestea, sweetener, nutmeg, and pumpkin pie spice. Pour in boiling water. Stir. Add orange juice. *Delicious.* One serving.

Calories/**126**

Tomato Bouillon

½ cup tomato juice
½ cup bouillon (any flavor)

Combine tomato juice and bouillon; heat in a saucepan. One serving.

Calories/**20**

Spiced Hot Tomato Toddy

½ cup tomato juice
Pinch nutmeg and cinnamon
½ cup unsweetened orange juice
Thin slice orange (for garnish)

In a saucepan, combine tomato juice, nutmeg, and cinnamon; bring to boil. Add orange juice. Pour into mug and garnish with the orange slice. One serving.

Calories/**74**

Tomato Refresher

2½ cups tomato juice
3 tablespoons lemon juice
⅛ teaspoon celery salt
1 teaspoon Worcestershire sauce
Thin slices lemon (for garnish)

Combine tomato juice, lemon juice, celery salt, and Worcestershire sauce. Chill. Stir before serving and garnish with thin lemon slices. Serves 5.

Calories per serving/**12**
(1 cup)

Low-Calorie Cocoa

1 cup skim milk
1 teaspoon unsweetened dry cocoa powder
Non-caloric sweetener, to taste

In a saucepan, warm skim milk, unsweetened dry cocoa powder, and sweetener. Stir frequently to prevent scorching. One serving.

Calories/**94**

Orange Petal

¾ cup skim milk
¼ cup unsweetened reconstituted orange juice
1-2 drops almond extract
Non-caloric sweetener, to taste

Mix skim milk, orange juice, almond extract, and sweetener. Beat or shake until well-mixed. Pour over ice cubes and serve. One serving.

Calories/**188**

Baked Apple

1 medium apple
1¼ teaspoon seedless raisins
2 tablespoons apple juice
2 teaspoons brown sugar
¾ cup Fresca

Core apple and fill cavity with raisins. Sprinkle brown sugar on top. Slowly pour a small amount of Fresca into cored apple. Pour remainder of raisins and Fresca in bottom of baking dish. Bake in 350° oven until tender, or cover lightly and microwave 2 minutes. One serving.

Calories/**129**

Fruit Kabob

Pineapple chunks
Melon chunks
Strawberry slices
Orange slices
Mint leaves (for garnish)

On skewer, alternate pineapple, melon, strawberries, and orange slices. Serve with cottage cheese or include chunks of cheese on skewer. Garnish with fresh mint leaves. One serving.

Calories/**Vary**
(according to fruits and cheeses used)

Banana Whip Shake

1 frozen banana
6 ounces skim milk
1 teaspoon vanilla
¼ cup orange juice (optional)

In blender, crush banana 1 minute. Add rest of ingredients and blend 1 minute more. *Delicious.* One serving.

Calories per serving:
With orange juice/**208**
Without orange juice/**180**

Party Banana Split

2 red apples
2 bananas
1 No. 303 can fruit cocktail, no sugar added
2 No. 303 cans chunk pineapple (juice-packed)
2 6-ounce can mandarin orange slices, drained
Dash cinnamon
¼ cup dry roasted peanuts

Core apples (leave peels on); cut into chunks. Peel 1
banana; cut into slices. Combine apple chunks, banana
slices, fruit cocktail, pineapple chunks, orange slices, and
cinnamon. Toss until mixed. Refrigerate. To serve, line a
platter with lettuce. Mound fruit mixture over lettuce.
Sprinkle peanuts on top. Peel other banana and cut lengthwise into strips. Arrange around salad.

Calories per serving/**100**
(1 cup)

Summertime Celebration

2 cups watermelon balls
2 cups fresh strawberries
1 cup sliced fresh peaches
1 cup seedless green grapes
2 tablespoons lime juice

Lightly toss all ingredients. Serve in sherbet glasses with
sprig of mint leaf for garnish.

Calories per serving/**120**
(1 cup)

Fruit Glory

3 cups chopped apples
2 cups sliced oranges
2 cups sliced strawberries
2 No. 303 cans chunk pineapple (juice-packed)
2 tablespoons lemon juice

In deep bowl, cut apples. Sprinkle lemon juice over the apple chunks to prevent them from turning brown. Add oranges and strawberries. Drain pineapple and add. Pour in pineapple juice as desired. *Eat and enjoy to the glory of the Lord.*

Calories per serving/**134**
(1 cup)

Pineapple Dessert

1 cup buttermilk
1 cup crushed pineapple (juice-packed)
1 cup Cool Whip
Sweetener, to taste

Gently mix all ingredients and fold into round cake pan. Freeze. Let stand a few minutes, then cut into 8 pieces. Fruit may be spooned over each plate as it is served. Serves 8.

Calories per serving/**52**
(Add extra calories for fruit:)

Grape Dessert

Small bunch seedless grapes,
  washed and separated
½ cup low-calorie cottage cheese

Mix grapes and cottage cheese. Pour into sauce dish.
One serving.

Calories/**147**

Amazing Apple Jello

2 cups unsweetened apple juice
1 package unsweetened gelatin

Heat apple juice until it comes to a boil. Pour into bowl
over gelatin. Mix until gelatin is dissolved. Chill until
thickened. Fruit may be added before it is completely
thickened. Serves 4.

Calories per serving/**64**
(½ cup. Add calories for fruit.)

Lo-Cal Gel-O

1 12-ounce can frozen fruit juice, thawed
  (Apple, grape, and cranberry make a clear Gel-O.)
2 packets unflavored gelatin
1½ cups boiling water

Soften gelatin in juice. Add to boiling water. Stir until
clear. Chill. Stir in fruit or vegetables before the Gel-O
sets.

Calories/**Vary**
*(Add calories for all ingredients
and divide by number of servings.)*

Summer Blueberry Yum

½ cup low-calorie Vanilla Frozen Dessert
½ cup diet lemon-lime soda
½ cup blueberries

Put frozen dessert into a goblet and mix in soda with a fork until slushy. Carefully stir in the blueberries. *Enjoy!*
One serving.

Calories/**145**

Baked Apple

1 green or red apple
1 tablespoon orange juice
Cinnamon, to taste

Core apple (do not cut in ½). Place in a small dish or baking pan. Drizzle with orange juice and sprinkle cinnamon on top. Microwave on "high" for 5-6 minuts, depending upon the size of the apple, or bake in the oven at 375° for 40 minutes. One serving.

Calories/**60**

Peach Cobbler

1 slice bread, crumbled
1 peach, peeled and sliced
Cinnamon, to taste
1 cup nonfat milk, scalded
1 egg
¼ teaspoon vanilla

Arrange bread crumbles in a shallow baking dish (4-6 inches in diameter). Arrange peach slices over the bread and sprinkle with cinnamon. Pour scalded milk into blender. Add egg and vanilla. Immediately blend at high speed for 30 seconds. Pour milk mixture over peach and bread. Lift up a few bread crumbles to form a top crust. Bake at 350° for 25-30 minutes, until top crust is browned and cobbler is set. (Do not cook the cobbler in a microwave oven because the egg mixture will curdle.) Let the cobbler stand 5 minutes to cool. *This can be eaten for breakfast or as a dessert.* Serves 2.

Calories per serving/**135**

Almond Meringue Cookies

4 egg whites
⅔ cup nonfat dry milk
1 teaspoon vanilla extract
1 teaspoon almond extract
Sweetener, to taste
Cinnamon, to taste

Beat egg whites until stiff. Fold in milk and mix well. Add extracts and sweetener. Spoon-drop onto cookie sheet. Bake in 275° oven 45 minutes. Remove from sheet and dust with cinnamon. Yield: 4 dozen cookies.

Calories per serving/**10**
(2 cookies)

Fruit Bars

1 cup water
1 cup raisins
2 apples, peeled and chopped
¼ cup shortening
2 tablespoons liquid sweetener
1 teaspoon cinnamon
¼ teaspoon nutmeg
1 egg
1 teaspoon vanilla
½ teaspoon black walnut flavoring or ½ cup nutmeats
1 cup flour
1 teaspoon baking soda
¼ teaspoon salt

Combine water, raisins, apples, shortening, sweetener, cinnamon, and nutmeg. Boil 3 minutes. Cool. Beat egg; add vanilla flavoring (or nutmeats). Add flour, baking soda, and salt. Stir the 2 mixtures together. Spread in a 9×9-inch pan. Bake at 350° for 25 minutes. Yield: 25 bars.

Calories per serving/**76**
(1 bar)

"I run to win! I train with aim!
I fight with victory in my sight!"

Pina Colada Squares

4 envelopes unflavored gelatin (If only 2 envelopes
   gelatin are used, it's more like pudding. Good!)
2½ cups unsweetened pineapple juice, heated to boiling
1 cup vanilla ice milk or Nice 'N Lite
2 tablespoons flaked coconut
⅛ teaspoon rum extract

In medium bowl, mix gelatin with sweetener. Add hot
juice and stir until gelatin is completely dissolved. Stir in
remaining ingredients. Blend thoroughly. Pour into 8- or
9-inch square baking pan and chill until firm. Cut into
1-inch squares. Yield: 6 dozen squares.

Calories per serving/**15**
(1 square)

Strawberry Pie

Meringue Crust
3 egg whites
1 teaspoon baking powder
Sweetener equal to ½ cup sugar
10 soda crackers, finely crushed
½ cup chopped nuts

Preheat oven to 300°. Whip egg whites until they stand
in peaks that lean over slightly when the beater is removed.
Beat in 1 teaspoon at a time: baking powder, sweetener,
soda crackers, and chopped nuts. PAM-spray a 10-inch
pie plate (include edges) and pour in meringue. Spread
meringue out to the edges, leaving a hollow in the center.
Make sure meringue is up to the top edge of the pie plate.
Bake in a 300° oven 30 minutes. Cool thoroughly (crust
will crack). *It's delicious.*

Strawberry Filling

1-2 cups sliced strawberries (or other berries, or peaches)
1 8-ounce carton Cool Whip

Mix berries and Cool Whip. Just before serving, pour into meringue crust. *(Doesn't keep well.)* Serves 8.

Calories per serving/**95**

Orange Dip

1 cup Mock Sour Cream (See recipe on page 58.)
1-2 teaspoons grated orange rind

Mix ingredients. Chill, and dip (for fresh fruit).

Calories per serving/**13**
(1 tablespoon)

Glorious Fruit Cup

2 cups fresh strawberries, washed and hulled
½ medium pineapple, diced
2 medium apples, cored and diced
2 small oranges, chopped
2 tablespoons lemon juice
2 tablespoons vanilla extract

Combine strawberries, diced pineapple, diced apples, and chopped oranges. Combine lemon juice and vanilla; pour over fruit. Turn mixture over twice. Place ⅛ mixture in sherbet glass. Repeat with remaining mixture. Serves 8.

Calories per serving/**58**

Bran Muffins

1 cup All-Bran
½ cup shortening
1 cup honey, molasses, or sorghum
2 eggs, beaten
2 cups buttermilk
2½ cups whole-wheat flour
3 teaspoons baking soda
½ teaspoon salt
½ teaspoon vanilla
2 cups 40% Bran Flakes or raw wheat germ
1 cup boiling water

Pour the boiling water over the All-Bran. Let stand while creaming the shortening and sweetening together. Add the 2 beaten eggs, then the soaked bran. Mix in the buttermilk. Add the remaining dry ingredients and vanilla. Bake in greased muffin pans or cupcake papers 20-30 minutes at 400°. If overbaked the muffins tend to be dry and crumbly. Nuts or dried fruits may be added or the top sprinkled with cinnamon.

Calories per serving/**160**
*(1 muffin; add calories for
any additions to recipe)*

*"Immediate VICTORY is more important
than immediate results!"*

Bran Muffins

2 cups whole-wheat flour
4 teaspoons baking powder
¾ teaspoon salt
2 cups bran
1 tablespoon melted butter
¾ cup sunflower seeds
1 egg, well-beaten
½ cup honey
1¼ cup skim milk

Sift dry ingredients together. Stir in bran and nuts. Add remaining ingredients and stir only until moistened. Fill 18 muffin cups equally. Bake at 400°-425° for 25-35 minutes.

Calories per serving/**113**
(1 muffin)

Thin 'n Crispy Sweet Bread

2 eggs
2 tablespoons Brown Sugar Twin
¼ teaspoon salt substitute (regular, unseasoned)
1 teaspoon vanilla extract

In mixing bowl, beat ingredients until mixed. Spray large *unheated* Teflon pan generously with PAM. Cover bottom of *unheated* pan evenly with egg mixture. Turn heat to "medium." After mixture has little bubbles and is completely solid, carefully turn to heat other side. Turning occasionally, heat until browned and partially crisped. *Cut it any way you like, and enjoy!* One serving.

Calories/**165**

Sugar Content of Cereals

Research was conducted at the Nutrient Composition Laboratory of the Agriculture Research Center, located in Beltsville, Maryland (1980), on 62 cereals. Analysis showed that cereal manufacturers add far more sucrose (table sugar) than any other sugar. Other sugars added are lactose from milk, milk chocolate, or milk powder; maltose from added corn syrup; and fructose and glucose that occur naturally in raisins (therefore products containing raisins had these sugars at considerably higher levels).

CEREALS CONTAINING 40% OR MORE SUGAR

Sugar Smacks	55%	Frosted Rice Krinkles	42%
Apple Jacks	54%	Fruity Pebbles	42%
Froot Loops	54%	Lucky Charms	41%
Sugar Corn Pops	46%	Cookie Crisp,	
Super Sugar Crisp	46%	Chocolate Chip	41%
Crazy Cow, Chocolate	46%	Crazy Cow,	
Frankenberry	45%	Strawberry	41%
Cocoa Krispies	44%	Captain Crunch	40%
Cap'n Crunch	44%	Cookie Crisp,	
Crunchberries	44%	Oatmeal	40%
Cocoa Pebbles	43%	Sugar Frosted Flakes	40%
Cookie Crisp, Vanilla	43%	Quisp	40%

CEREALS CONTAINING 39% TO 25% SUGAR

Count Chocula	39%	Raisin Bran (17% from	
Alphabits	38%	raisins)	30%
Honey Combs	38%	Golden Grahams	30%
Frosted Rice	37%	Cracklin' Bran	30%
Trix	36%	C. W. Post	28%
Coca Puffs	35%	Frosted Mini Wheats	26%
Cap'n Crunch,			
Peanut Butter	32%		

CEREALS CONTAINING 24% TO 10% SUGAR

Country Crisp	22%	Life	17%
Life, Cinnamon	22%	Team	14%
100% Bran	21%	40% Bran Flakes	13%
All Bran	19%	Grape Nuts Flakes	13%
Fortified Oat Flakes	18%	Buckwheats	12%

CEREALS CONTAINING LESS THAN 10% SUGAR

Concentrate	9%	Post Toasties	5%
Product 19	9%	Kix	5%
Total	8%	Rice Chex	4%
Wheaties	8%	Cheerios	3%
Grape Nuts	7%	Wheat or Corn Chex	3%
Rice Krispies	7%	Shredded Wheat	1%
Special K	6%	Puffed Wheat or Rice	1%
Corn Flakes	6%		

Food Facts

Limit These Protein Foods
Lean beef, pork, lamb, to
  1 pound per week total
Eggs to 4 per week
Hard cheese to 4 ounces
  per week

High Vitamin C Fruits (no sugar added)
1 medium orange
½ medium mango
4 ounces grapefruit juice
4 ounces orange juice
½ medium cantaloupe

½ medium grapefruit
1 cup strawberries
1 large tangerine
8 ounces tomato juice

Other Fruits (no sugar added)
1 medium apple or peach
½ cup pineapple
½ round slice water-
  melon (1"×10")
1 small banana or pear
½ cup berries

½ small honeydew melon
¼ pound cherries or
  grapes
2-3 apricots, prunes,
  or plums
2 tablespoons raisins

High Vitamin A Vegetables
Broccoli
Carrots
Chicory
Escarole

Mustard greens, collards
  and other leafy greens
Pumpkin
Winter squash
Watercress

Potato or Substitute
1 medium potato
1 small sweet potato
  or yam
½ cup cooked brown
  rice

1 small ear corn
½ cup corn or green
  lima beans, peas
½ cup cooked dry
  beans, peas, lentils

Fat
1 teaspoon safflower oil
1 teaspoon mayonnaise
2 teaspoons French
  dressing
1 teaspoon butter

1 teaspoon margarine
  with liquid vegetable
  oil listed first on label
  of ingredients

Skim Milk or Substitute
2 cups (8 ounces each)
  buttermilk
⅔ cup nonfat dry milk
  solids

1 cup (8 ounces)
  evaporated skim milk

You May Drink

Coffee Tea Water Club Soda Bouillon Consomme

You May Use

Salt Pepper Herbs Spices Lemon/Lime Horseradish Vinegar

You May Eat Freely

Asparagus
Green and wax beans
Broccoli
Brussels sprouts
Carrots
Cauliflower
Celery
Chicory
Collards
Cucumber
Dandelion greens
Escarole
Kale
Lettuce
Mustard greens
Parsley
Romaine lettuce
Spinach
Summer squash
Swiss chard
Tomato
Turnip greens
Watercress

Try to Avoid (or at least limit severely)

Bacon, fatty meats,
    sausage
Beer, liquor, wines
Butter, margarine (other
    than described above)
Cakes, cookies, crackers
Doughnuts, pastries, pies
Candy, chocolates, nuts
Whole milk
Muffins, pancakes,
    waffles
Yogurt (fruit-flavored)
Cream—sweet and sour
Cream cheese, non-dairy
    cream substitutes
French fried potatoes,
    potato chips
Pizza, popcorn, pretzels
    and similar snacks
Olives
Soda (both diet and
    sugar-sweetened)
Gelatin desserts, pud-
    dings (both diet and
    sugar-sweetened)
Gravies and sauces
Honey, jams, jellies,
    sugar and syrup
Ice cream, ices, ice milk,
    sherbets, frozen yogurt
Spaghetti, macaroni,
    noodles

Complete Recipe Listing

Vegetables

Desserts and Beverages